Addressing Common Homeschool Misconceptions

The Truths Behind Homeschool Myths

Donna Goff   Julia Groves

MAGNITUDE

DEDICATION

To all the parents who have had to face opposition to their choice to homeschool. Remember most opposition is based in the belief in homeschool misconceptions. When you are armed with the truth you can address the misconceptions of your friends and family and homeschool with confidence .

BOOKS IN THE HOMESCHOOLING BASICS SERIES

A Beginner's Guide for Homeschooling:
How to Set Up a Successful Homeschool

Answers to The Top Homeschooling Questions:
Helping Parent's Homeschool With Confidence

Addressing Common Homeschool Misconceptions:
The Truths Behind Homeschool Myths

CONTENTS

Addressing Common Homeschool Misconceptions

INTRODUCTION

This is book three in our *Homeschooling Basics Series*. In book, 1 *A Beginner's Guide for Homeschooling*, we talked about how to set up a successful homeschool by making sure you have a solid foundation. Then in book 2, *Answers to the Top Homeschooling Questions* we sought to provide detailed answers about how to go about homeschooling in today's world.

In this book, we are going to address those common myths and misconceptions that have surrounded homeschooling for the last several decades.

We can't tell you how many times over the years we have been presented with these same homeschool misconceptions by friends who were "Concerned" with our decision to homeschool. Being armed with the truth behind these misconceptions has helped us to move forward and homeschool in confidence and without fear.

Before we jump in and start addressing these popular homeschool myths and misconceptions, we would like to take a moment to introduce ourselves and our homeschooling background.

Hi, I am Donna Goff and I began homeschooling in the 1980s. Before I had children, I had never planned to homeschool. So, when I came to homeschooling, I did so reluctantly. It was before the internet and so I only had bookstores and libraries as my sources to figure it out. There were no support groups within about eighty miles! Because homeschooling was not my plan, I had no real plan except to pick up where they left off. I learned the hard way that this is not how to go about beginning homeschooling. This lack of planning resulted in my older children being in and out of public school.

My story would be really short, had I firmly settled earlier on whether to either homeschool or public school. If I had it to do over, I would homeschool all of my children from the beginning, through high school, and not just my younger four children. I share my story, because I feel it pertains a lot to this book, to know my journey. I write this in hopes that you will benefit from my experiences.

When I only had two sons and a daughter, I found myself drawn into the early learning philosophy. I took a live week long detailed course in early childhood development. It was focused on how to enhance my children's development and early learning.

The things I learned during that time have benefited all of my children. However, a lot of the early learning I found to be too tedious or not natural, as they involved flash cards. I did take the principles of clear focused repetition into my life and in teaching my children. When my daughter was two, we tried doing a play based preschool. All the moms wanted to add academics. As we did not know any better, we added academics. We did preschool for one semester.

Later, I had four more children, but armed with more information, I chose not to do preschool at home, nor did I send my children to preschool. I focused more on providing support for healthy development.

My older three children attended kindergarten. I had no idea the law did not require it in the state where I lived. In talking to the principal, he suggested I homeschool! I gave him my notice and two weeks later I started homeschooling my oldest, he was in fourth grade.

We moved and by Christmas I was homeschooling all of them, kinder, third, and fourth grade. That summer I had my fourth child and because of this sent my oldest children back to public school where they attended for the next two years. I had my fifth child and decided to try homeschooling my children again. However, before long, I was exhausted and sleep deprived from a newborn. My husband re-enrolled our older children in public school. I must say I felt guilty and felt like I had failed.

We moved to Utah. I enrolled my three oldest children in public school. However, a few months later my daughter begged to just be homeschooled. I understood why she requested to be homeschooled, so I agreed to her request. As we left the school that day, we walked by the kindergarten classroom. I pointed it out to her younger sister who replied, "That's fine for them mom, I have something better."

At that instant, I realized I was into homeschooling for the long haul. I invested time in learning about models, philosophies, methods, and connecting with other homeschoolers. I had my sixth child.

My oldest two, who didn't want to be homeschooled, chose to do independent study and graduated from high school early. I then had a seventh child. My oldest daughter was homeschooled from sixth grade through graduation. My youngest four children were homeschooled to adulthood.

In this book, I want to share from my experience and help you to begin your homeschool journey. Starting out right, can mean a world of difference in how your homeschool flows.

Hi, my name is Julia Groves (I am Donna Goff's oldest daughter). As my mother previously stated, my first personal experience with homeschooling was when I was in kindergarten when my parents, for a brief time, pulled my older brothers out of the public school system (due to issues at their school) and opted to homeschool them. I enjoyed joining in on their studies. I have a particular memory from that time of my father teaching my older brothers and I how to add large numbers together. He taught us on this huge white board. I remember feeling so grown up that I knew how to add really big numbers together.

Anyway, while that was my first homeschool experience, my official homeschool journey didn't begin for several more years. It began in the middle of my sixth grade year. That is when I begged my mother, one day, to let me come home to be homeschooled full time. There were a number of reasons for this personal request. The main one being, I had no desire to skip another grade (which was being discussed), as I was getting bullied enough, for having already done so at my last school.

I decided that I wanted to come home and take charge of my own education. I wanted to really study the subjects I was interested in, rather than just skimming the surface, as we were doing in school. I wanted peace away from all the bullies. My mother, seeing the writing on the wall, agreed to my request and that's how I ended up being homeschooled from the sixth-grade year through high school. (Though I did take a few classes at our local highschool with my friends. I even performed in a school play at our local highschool thanks to the kindness of an understanding drama teacher)

Looking back, I have never regretted my decision to be homeschooled, even though it came with its own set of trials. The main one being that homeschooling wasn't as widespread or accepted back then. So, I got a lot of push back from my friends and their parents. No, I never doubted or regretted my choice to be homeschooled. In fact, I am very grateful I had the opportunity.

Later on, after attending a couple semesters at private liberal arts college, I taught for a short time at private elementary school, before stepping away from formally teaching, in order to raise my own family. However, through the years, I have enjoyed speaking at various Homeschool conferences to both youth and adults.

Now, I have three kids of my own who I am currently homeschooling, together with my husband. I have to say that homeschooling isn't always the easiest educational choice, but it can be the most rewarding. I love teaching my kids and learning from them. But what I really love is that the world is our school. We can go anywhere and learn as we go. We have freedom.

All, right. It's time to talk about those oh so common Homeschool Myths and Misconceptions surrounding Homeschooling.

.

Addressing Common Homeschool Misconceptions

1. MISCONCEPTION: HOMESCHOOLING IS CHILD ABUSE

Plain and simple, homeschooling is NOT a form of child abuse. Many of the people who believe in this misconception are often very vocal about their belief. They lobby to either make homeschooling illegal, as it is in some countries, or call for a lot more government oversight in regards to homeschooling.

We are addressing this misconception first, because in reality, it's foundation is based in the belief in many, if not all of the misconceptions we will address in the following chapters. These chapter titles and subtitles are not our opinion, but the misconceptions that we will address.

Those who believe that homeschooling is child abuse, often believe that homeschool children are neglected. They believe that homeschool children are disadvantaged, because they don't have the same access to facilities, certified teachers and social interaction. Many of these people believe that homeschool children aren't being taught, and that the children just play all day. They believe that homeschool children fall behind their peers in school, and won't be able to get into college, or get work later in life. Some just have a different worldview and assume their worldview will only be addressed in school.

There are some who believe that homeschool parents actually physically and emotionally abuse their children. They believe that because there is not a lot of oversight, that there is no way to catch abuse when happening to homeschooled children.

Abuse is awful, and sadly, it happens in our society. Sometimes abuse happens in homeschool families, but most homeschool families are not abusive.

Abuse happens at home to children who attend public school, and is often missed or left unaddressed by their overseers.

Sadly, a lot of abuse happens at school. Verbal abuse, emotional abuse, and physical abuse come from peers at school. According to government statistics, about 20% of public school children feel bullied by other school children. Many children are impacted by this throughout their lives, whether they are the victim, the bully, or an observer. Even when schools claim zero tolerance for bullying, a lot of peer bullying happens.

Some children are bullied, shamed, and treated disrespectfully by some teachers. We have all seen the cartoons of the child in the corner with a dunce cap on. We have heard of teachers whacking children with rulers. Fortunately, that is something that has been banned. And some children abuse their teachers.

In recent years, both teachers and coaches have been implicated in child sexual abuse scandals. The oversight of being at school did nothing protect these children. Yet, we cannot vilify every school teacher, coach, or home because a few abusers.

Those who are truly concerned about child abuse, need to focus on child abuse everywhere, not just hunting for the needle in the haystack, in focusing only on the 2 -3 % of children who are homeschooled, and looking for only for child abuse there. They should be addressing the real elephant in the room.

When one in five school children experience peer abuse, and others experience abuse from adults at school, there is a large abuse problem in our schools. This is where an overwhelming majority of children spend their childhood, in compulsory schooling.

HOMESCHOOL FAMILIES SHOULD BE REPORTED TO SOCIAL SERVICES

Homeschool is not abuse and should not be reported, as such.

Child abuse is real in this world. It happens no matter where children are educated, regardless of oversight. While most parents, coaches, and teachers are not abusers, some are.

If you see actual abuse, then report it. Just know that the vast majority of over two million homeschool families are not neglectful or abusive. Homeschool children usually outperform their public school peers and grow to be socially, well adjusted adults.

There was a time in America that neighbors who did not agree with the idea of homeschooling, reported their homeschooling neighbors as child abusers. Many states tied up a lot of time and money to investigate these families. Since then, many states have changed their laws to prevent this.

You CANNOT report a neighbor for homeschooling, citing homeschooling as child abuse. Why? Homeschooling has been legal in all fifty states, since 1993. States were usually not finding child abuse or neglect in the homes reported for homeschooling.

Child protective agencies need to spend time and resources in addressing real abuse and real neglect. This is an excellent article by HSLDA "If You Suspect Abuse." This article talks about the difference between intentional harm to a child and challenges that parents can face that can be remedied. (https://hslda.org/post/if-you-suspect-child-abuse)

WHAT TO DO IF SOCIAL SERVICES IS CALLED?

Be proactive. Before you begin homeschooling, make sure you know your state laws. We discuss this in our first book in the **Homeschooling Basics** series - *A Beginner's Guide to Homeschooling.*

1. Understand your state's homeschool laws.

2. Create your homeschool business plan.

3. Make sure you comply with your state's homeschool laws.

4. Pay attention to home culture. Little messes are expected with children, then help them learn to clean them up.

    However, general filth, trash on the floors, days worth of dirty dishes, dirty clothes all over, can be a sign of neglect and will raise flags.

5. Homeschool!

6. Keep good homeschool records. A daily learning log is simple and easy to keep.

7. Keep a portfolio for each child, showing their progress.

8. In good times, build community and develop friends in the homeschooling community. Be willing to help one another. Sometimes illness, finances, personal or local disasters can negatively impact the children, homeschool, and the running of a home. These things

can leave a family in chaos. There is no shame in reaching out for help.

It would be a good idea to check the Homeschool Legal Defense Association website (https://hslda.org/). Check out the membership in HSLDA. We are not affiliated. They keep up on the latest state laws, give homeschool advice on their site, and defend homeschoolers in court.

Be proactive!

2. MISCONCEPTION: HOMESCHOOLED CHILDREN ARE SOCIALLY INEPT

The question of socialization always seems to come up when discussing homeschooling. Probably, because the idea that most homeschooled children are socially inept is a persistent and common misconception. Which is why we have written about this subject in both of our previous books, *A Beginner's Guide for Homeschooling & Answers to the Top Homeschool Questions.*

We are sure there are some socially inept homeschoolers, as there are socially inept children that emerge from public schools, public charters, and private schools.

Admittedly, some homes do a poor job of inculcating good social skills. Some of those children are home schooled, some are public schooled, and some are schooled in private school. However, as research shows, social ineptitude is not the norm for homeschoolers.

CHILDREN NEED TO SPEND 6-7 HOURS A DAY WITH OTHER CHILDREN OUTSIDE OF THEIR FAMILY TO BE WELL ROUNDED

Many assume that children must be in school (all day, five days a week) with a group of children their own age, to be properly socialized. The implication is that children in public, public charter and private schools are being properly socialized, by their peers. While children that are homeschooled, are not given the opportunity to be "socialized" in the like manner.

As a result, many believe that homeschoolers could not possibly get enough varied social interaction. Nothing could be further from the truth.

Yes, it is true that some social skills can be developed in the classroom and on the playground, at school. However, those are not the only places that social skills can be learned.

It is in the home, that children receive their first lessons in social skills. Treating others respectfully, taking turns in conversations, learning the art of conversation, learning to assert ourselves, sharing, negotiating, respecting elders and more, can be learned in the home.

Even when there are no other children in the home, children who are homeschooled usually have access to associate with neighborhood children, and opportunities for regular social contact with varied ages, in and outside the home.

HOMESCHOOL DOESN'T OFFER THE OPPORTUNITIES NEEDED FOR YOUR CHILD TO DEVELOP IMPORTANT SOCIAL SKILLS

The truth of that matter is, that homeschool children often have more social opportunities, than conventionally schooled children have.

In school, there are fewer opportunities for broad and diverse social contact, than most realize. At schools, children are placed in a classroom with same-aged peers. Field trips are few and far between. Interacting with other ages, other than the teacher, is also more rare.

Likewise, the social opportunities available to homeschool children are much more broad, than is commonly thought. Homeschooled children live together and interact with siblings and parents. Also, homeschool children can interact with people of all ages in their neighborhood and community. And for those homeschoolers that are travel schoolers, the world is their community and school.

In most areas of the United States, there are large homeschool organizations. Some organize group field trip discounts. Homeschool parents in other areas, create their own homeschool choir.

In many areas, homeschool organizations offer special interest classes and group activities for homeschoolers. Other homeschoolers enjoy community activities along with children who are not homeschooled.

HOMESCHOOL CHILDREN DON'T KNOW HOW TO HANDLE CONFLICT RESOLUTION OR WORK WELL WITH PEERS

To begin with, conflict resolution skills are at first taught and caught at home, not at school. Siblings must learn how to resolve their conflicts on a daily basis.

Children learn conflict resolution skills while working and playing together, as siblings, and with parents.

This is one reason, we encourage family work, no matter where children are educated. As children work together in the home, they learn conflict resolution skills. These are skills that are not taught when children fly solo, doing chores in their own bubble.

Aside from in grade school and junior high schools, where in adult life are people grouped only with people their own age? Contemporary mass schooling is arranged, by age, for convenience in graduating at eighteen. This age grouping has no useful purpose, in adult life.

High school courses have children of all high school ages in them. For those going to college, they may find people in their classes old enough to be their parents.

It is imperative for children to have opportunities to interact with multi-aged groups of people. We live and work in a multi-aged world.

HOMESCHOOL CHILDREN WILL BE WEIRD

Usually, children are as weird as their family is, no matter where they are educated. Let's face it, we all knew some pretty weird children we attended school with. Like the one who ate glue, or stuck pencils up their nose. Not to mention the bullies.

Julia- *True stories: When I was in public school, in first grade, there were a bunch of older kids who came around the playground. They accused us first graders, in a horrified way, of being a virgin. To which all the first graders would say, "Nuhah. I'm not a virgin."*

In my second grade class, there were two kids who spent half their class time painting their hands and arms with elmer's glue. every day. They did this so they could peel it off when it dried, and have a second skin to play with for the rest of class.

Later in third grade, a bunch of guys, on spaghetti lunch days, thought it was so cool to swallow the long noodles and then gag themselves. Then the noodles would come out their nose. Then they would floss their tonsils with the noodles.

In fifth grade (I skipped fourth), it was the popular thing to do to push your eyelids inside out and walk around like that, grossing out the younger students.

Yeah, it's not homeschool children that are weird. It is children in general. However, if you are really worried about your children turning out MORE weird than normal, these are some things you can do. Evaluate your social strengths. What are areas you can improve in? Your example and the environment you create in your home, can go a long way in helping your children become decent human beings. You can model, teach, and expect decent behavior in the home.

Invite others into your life and into your home. These varied social experiences will broaden your children.

Read aloud to your family from great literature. The study of great literature can be very instructive in the different aspects of human nature. Literature can also inform children about what is socially acceptable action. Discuss the literature and principles learned there.

HOMESCHOOLED CHILDREN WILL BE ANTISOCIAL

To be anti-social, is to be against society's norms. Being antisocial is not the norm for most people, including the homeschool community. If you look, you may find some, but that is atypical.

You will also find antisocial children in the public school. However, that again is not the norm there either.

Also, consider, that there may be some social trends in society that are worth not embracing. Know that you can do so and not be antisocial.

HOMESCHOOL CHILDREN ARE GOING TO BE LONELY

While there may be some homeschooled children that are lonely, it is not necessarily because they are homeschooled. There are also children in public school that are lonely, though they are surrounded by peers. Oftentimes, loneliness can be attributed to shyness and social anxiety. It can also be due to not fitting in with the crowd.

If your child suffers from feeling lonely, then there are things you can do, as parents, to be proactive to address the issue.

We would advise you to be a part of your child's life, outside of providing home education for them. Children who are actively engaged with their parents, siblings, and extended family are usually not lonely. When was the last time you got down and played with your children, like actually played?

For older children this could be pulling out favorite board and card games. For younger children play often involves physical activity or imaginative play with favorite dolls, toys and stuffed animals. Additionally, think about family walks, movie nights, and one-on-one parent/child dates.

Some parents provide activities or classes, in their homes. This draws in other homeschoolers for more interaction with their children. Some provide after school activities. Others look for activities within the homeschool community and join in. You can also apply this to non-homeschooled friends and family.

However, whatever you choose, do not go overboard and let these activities take over your life.

Many children also have distance friends. Penpals are a traditional method of connecting with children all over the world. Now with the internet, there are cyber pals, as well. There are safe programs that even allow children to video call each other, over the internet at no additional cost to parents.

HOMESCHOOL CHILDREN DON'T GET PROPER EXERCISE AND ARE OFTEN OVERWEIGHT

Homeschool children, like their public school counterparts, come in all shapes and sizes.

Actually, more can be done at home, than in schools to promote real health. Many schools are cutting recess. Many children at home and in school spend far too many hours sitting in front of screens. Moms, you can have a positive impact on the health and lifestyles of your children.

At home, you can feed your children healthy balanced meals that you know your children will actually eat. You can also choose to limit or not buy a lot of junk food. You can encourage adequate hydration in between meals and provide healthy snack options.

As a homeschool parent, you can take your children on regular long walks. You can do family exercises and meditations before academics in the morning. You can also choose healthy bedtimes at night, because you do not have to worry about staying up late, to finish school projects or homework.

In your homeschool, you can make sure to take "breather breaks" throughout the day, as needed. This can help your children to focus better during lesson time.

Did you know that Finland provides every grade school student with a fifteen minute non-negotiable recess, every hour in school?!? Recess is not held hostage to manipulate or incentivise children. Children cannot be kept in as a punishment. Nor are children held in to work with them longer. The time children are at school is finite and recess is vital. They do not have homework either. So, the teacher has only class time to work with the student.

Moms, you can do the same. You can rethink recess. Play is a non-negotiable essential for children. It is not an afterthought. It is important to their well being and progress. Children can do exercises, deep breathing, dance or take a walk/run around the block, as needed, in between subjects.

You can also limit school time, too. Gone are the hours of trying to get a child to complete work. When school time is over, take note, then close the book! Reducing stress can reduce the fight or flight response. Stress leads to obesity. Reducing the stress response can result in an increase in learning. Structure the time for learning, not how much teaching ground you will cover during that time.

Public school children and homeschooled children alike, have access to public playgrounds, trails, and sports facilities. Look for ways to be outside everyday.

If you do these things with your family, you probably won't have to worry about your children's weight or health.

Addressing Common Homeschool Misconceptions

3. MISCONCEPTION: PARENTS ARE NOT QUALIFIED TO HOMESCHOOL THEIR CHILDREN

In states where standardized testing is required of homeschoolers, the home schooled children typically test higher than conventionally schooled students. This is, even though the parents may not have an education degree or training.

There is an old Disney movie that we love called, *The One and Only, Genuine, Original Family Band*. In this movie, the family moves to a new territory, and the daughter is hired to be the new school teacher. The people in this area are so excited to have a teacher again. Their school had been closed down for far too long.

However, on the first day of school, the daughter was called in for a last minute school board meeting to show her credentials. She sends her grandfather to let the children at the school know that school wouldn't be starting that day after all, but the next day instead.

When the grandfather let the children know, many were upset. One girl in particular started crying, because she had worked hard to memorize a piece to recite for the new teacher. She had suffered sleeping with her hair in rags, to have curly hair the first day of school, which was now canceled.

Feeling bad for this little girl, the Grandfather told all the children that school wasn't canceled after all, and to get in their seats.

Why are we telling you this story? We are getting there…Ok, so the grandfather gets all the children into their seats, and had little Edna recite her poem from Ralph Waldo Emerson when a boy belligerently asks him, "Did you graduate from the 8th grade and do you have a certificate to show you are a regular qualified teacher?"

To which the grandfather responded, "I'll tell you this boy, If I know something you don't know then I am qualified to teach you. Provided of course that you have sense enough to learn." and then he began to teach.

We get so caught up in what we think is needed to be qualified to teach, that we lose sight of a simple truth. As adults with knowledge and experience, we have all the qualifications we need to teach our own children.

No one is better qualified to teach your children, than you, no matter how much formal knowledge they may have!

Why? For the simple fact that no one knows your children like you do. And no one cares as much about your children and their future, than you. Besides, you really don't need to know as much as you think, in order to teach.

YOU NEED A BACKGROUND IN TEACHING TO BE QUALIFIED TO HOMESCHOOL

There are some amazing, caring, and even gifted teachers working in the public, charter, and private schools. These teachers, in many cases, went through school and certification, to prepare them to teach in a school setting. They learned to use materials and methods designed to teach lots of children, in a classroom.

While these teachers have found their training very helpful to their work, this training is not necessary for homeschooling. As a homeschool parent teaching your children, you won't use many of the same skills these teachers have had to hone, to work with children in a classroom.

In the home, this is especially true, if you are teaching for mastery and not according to age-grade levels. For example, this can be done quite effectively, by teaching general knowledge together.

Why, together? Because general knowledge can be learned at any age, is not age specific, and not developmentally dependent. Then moms can do a break-out block of time to teach skills one-on-one. While mom is working one-on-one teaching skills in a mastery model, the other children can hone skills while working on projects of their interest.

Ironically, it is often the classroom teachers coming to homeschooling that struggle the most at first. Why? Their training is designed for the classroom. So, they come home, try to remake a room into a classroom, and set up schedules appropriate for the classroom. Once, they are at home, many begin making the shift, and do well at homeschooling. They always tell me though, that this was an adjustment!

Research by Dr. Brian D. Ray, Phd., at the National Home Education Research Institute, shows that about 10% of homeschool parents have teaching certification.

Homeschooled children, of parents who are certified teachers, generally score at the 87th percentile, compared to their school aged peers, who average at the 50th percentile.

 Homeschoolers typically score at the 88th percentile and 90% of those parents are not trained teachers.

Research has also shown that homeschoolers typically score 15-30 percentile points above their public school peers, on standardized tests. This is regardless of family income, race, or level of formal education, including homeschooled children of parents without a high school diploma!

YOU NEED TO HAVE A DEGREE OR BE REALLY REALLY "SMART" TO HOMESCHOOL

Homeschooling can seem daunting, in the beginning. Many people think that the more educated parents are, the easier it will be to homeschool. While higher education can help, it is not necessarily to have a degree, to be successful at homeschool.

Children from homes where mothers were high school dropouts, average in the lowest percentile in school. About 20% of homeschooled children are being homeschooled by parents without a high school diploma. Yet, children who are educated at home by parents who dropped-out average above the 80th percentile.

This may be due to homeschooling parents being more engaged with their children in education. While other parents may not feel qualified, and totally trust their child's education to the school.

Many homeschool parents have not used their grade school education, in real life. Because of this, they have either forgotten or had big gaps in their education. As they begin homeschooling, they find that they relearn, remember, or learn more, as they go.

HOMESCHOOLING REQUIRES SUBJECT MATTER KNOWLEDGE OF ALL SUBJECTS THAT WILL BE TAUGHT (ESPECIALLY IN HIGHER GRADES)

When teaching younger children in those early years, most of the skill knowledge should be easy for moms. These skills are the practical knowledge we use everyday.

Parents may feel ill equipped to teach general knowledge. However, many parents have discovered they can learn general knowledge along with their children.

One does not have to do a lot of prep time, if they use a grab and go, open and grow curriculum, such as Power of an Hour.

For older children, you can learn with them.

Donna- *When Julia was growing up, we took Beginning Hebrew together. Another homeschool mom and I wanted to learn Greek. So, we got a Greek tutor to meet with us once a week. I have taken Great Courses (videos with workbooks), and learned alongside my children.*

We have also assigned a topic for our youth to research. Then they came back and taught the rest of us the topic.

Learning, with the object of teaching others, is a powerful way to cement learning. Sometimes, they taught in hands-on ways. Other times they did presentations, becoming a historical figure, and teaching in first person.

WHAT IF YOU ARE WEAK IN AN AREA OF KNOWLEDGE?

Do you have a friend that has strength in that area? Perhaps they would be willing to teach that subject along with their own children. Just don't try to get too many of these going at the same time, as they can take over your homeschool day. This is not as nice as you might think.

The premise of homeschool co-ops. Co-ops can be beneficial, just be careful. Many parents join co-ops to simplify their life and the opposite happens. The classes take over their day and assignments reach into homeschool, and before they know it, homeschool is not happening. And the homeschool co-op usually meets only once a week. And then parents are back to having more commitments than they had when their children were in school.

So, tread lightly here, keep it simple and you won't regret it.

ONLY CERTAIN PERSONALITIES CAN HANDLE HOMESCHOOLING

Just as school teachers have different personalities, so do moms. Each personality type can be successful at homeschooling, just like parenting. The way they homeschool may differ by personality, but that's OK.

It is not always our personality that gets in the way. Too often, it is due to lack of information that results in unrealistic expectations. Moms may have to learn a little more about how children develop and learn. Then they can adjust expectations, to be able to work through challenges.

Often, new homeschool moms hit a wall in educating their children, and the children can become uncooperative. This is often the case, when moms try to recreate the classroom in the home. Especially so, if they begin to treat learning, the same way they treat domestic chores.

We do not advocate just handing young children a stack of assignments, domestic or academic. Nor do we encourage parents to manipulate with rewards and punishments, to get them to do those assignments. We want our children to have a love of learning and a love of work, to carry them forward in their learning. We discuss how to create a home culture, teach and motivate children to learn and work in our first book, *A Beginner's Guide for Homeschooling: How to Setup A Successful Homeschool.*

Many moms fear they might miss something in teaching, and just buy a bunch of workbooks and assign pages. Then they attach "incentives" to do the paperwork. This can be very overwhelming, not to mention uninspiring. Many children resist this, because they are being fit into a pace, instead of learning when their brains are ready.

If your child is resisting, this is a signal to stop and assess what is happening and why. With new information, moms are prepared to search for solutions. Then moms can make adjustments and move forward.

In the end, whether you are a highly structured mom or more naturally inclined mom, each personality can homeschool successfully. It will just look different from one home to the next which is a good thing.

YOU HAVE TO HAVE SAINT-LIKE PATIENCE TO HOMESCHOOL

One could argue that saint-like patience is a prerequisite of raising children, in general. Children sure do know how to push your buttons. They can be trying at times. This is natural, as they learn, grow, and mature.

The truth is, that while patience does come in handy, you don't have to be a saint to parent, or to homeschool. Thank goodness.

As with parenting, homeschooling, can refine us. We have found that our patience has grown over the years.

We are better parents because of the polishing that homeschooling brought to our lives. This, in turn, has grown our relationships with our children. As we came to challenges, we stopped, assessed, and worked through them, and we developed and matured together.

Know that you, your family, your home, and homeschool will be a continual work in progress. This is how life was designed to be.

PARENTS DON'T KNOW HOW TO TEACH CORRECTLY

We live in a society that is stuck on the idea that there is only one right way to do everything. From parenting, to school, to work and beyond. There are many so-called experts who will be quick to point out what you are doing "Wrong" and how to do things "Right."

The problem is, that in many instances, "Wrong" and "Right" ways to teach, are merely a matter of opinion. Which is why, time and again, this idea of there being only one way to properly teach things, has proven to be a false one. As the old adage goes, there is more than one way to skin a cat.

Just because your parenting and homeschool methods are different from someone else's, doesn't mean that you or that other person are doing it wrong. It just means you are doing it differently.

Parents may not be trained in classroom methods, but they have a lot of experience in training and working with their own children. Remember, classroom methods and materials were designed for the classroom. They were designed for when one teacher is working with several students to push them through to the next level.

Private tutors, governesses, and tutorial companies use different methods than classroom teachers. Methods and materials used in one-on-one and small group teaching are different than those used in the large classroom.

Parents working with their own children will not look the same as a classroom. By the time children enter school, parents have already taught their children to walk, talk, feed themselves, drink, and the rules of the house. Most parents have trained their children to do self-care. Many parents have taught their children family traditions. Often, moms have read to their children, taken them to the park, or enjoyed the zoo with their children. Most children learn their colors, to count, and learn many things, quite naturally, in the home, in the context of everyday living.

Just remember, you know your children better than anyone else. Trust in your instinct as a mother and go from there.

CHILDREN WON'T COOPERATE WITH THEIR PARENTS AS THEIR TEACHER

Children often do not cooperate with their teachers or their parents. We think they respond better to other adults, because we aren't there to see it. We assume our children are angels for other adults, unless we are told otherwise. At the end of the year, most children are advanced, to keep them with their agemates, not always because they earned it.

Have you struggled trying to get your children to do homework? Have you had a difficult time helping your children with homework? Take heart, homework is not homeschooling!

Many school children may feel powerless and overwhelmed. Often, they are simply not developmentally ready for the curriculum. They struggle in class because they are not ready. They do not learn it there, so they are assigned homework to reinforce what is being taught in class. This work is sent home, where parents get resistance, too. Many parents who have experienced this, come to the conclusion that their children will not cooperate with them. So, they feel they won't be able to homeschool their children.

Sadly, many children are just as overwhelmed by home expectations, too. Each day, they have spent about eight hours in school, then they come home to a pile of domestic and academic assignments.

Adults may think it is just a matter of obedience. The child just needs to buck up and do it. When in reality, what the child needs is habit training, and a parent working with them, at the child's pace. The child may not have enough maturity to fly solo, at this time.

If parents will step back, create their homeschool business plan, they will find better ways to work with their children. In *A Beginner's Guide for Homeschooling*, we show you how to assess and create your own plan, unique to your family and their needs.

4. MISCONCEPTION: HOMESCHOOLING IS ONLY OK IF DONE THE "RIGHT WAY"

We spoke about this in the last chapter. The idea that there is only one right way to homeschool is ridiculous.

Every child is different. Their personalities are different, how they learn and process information is different. Their needs are different.

That is why there is not a one-size fits-all for parenting. Also, parents have different personalities and different ways of teaching, that are more in line with what their children need, than a one-size fits-all method.

While there is no set "Right Way" to teach your children academics, there are certain foundational elements that most successful home schools have.

This is why, in book one of our *Homeschooling Basics Series, A Beginner's Guide for Homeschooling,* we talk to you about how to set up a successful home school, including finding the educational model, philosophy, and methods that resonate with you.

A HOMESCHOOL SHOULD BE A REPLICA OF A "REGULAR" SCHOOL CLASSROOM

Some moms have created beautiful, functional homeschool classrooms in their homes. We have seen a lot of really cute home school rooms. Pinterest and Instagram have lots of examples.

The idea behind creating an actual classroom in your home comes from the idea that it gives your children structure and stability. However, while these homeschool classrooms are both functional and beautiful, one can homeschool very well, without a classroom. Yes, many have found that it is not necessary for them to create a schoolroom in your home. Even tutorial businesses do not duplicate the public school classroom in their business model.

Donna- *We once had a cute, functional homeschool classroom, before we moved to Utah twenty-seven years ago, and no one used it. When our family bought a new home, it was decided to NOT spend money for a room to set aside for homeschool. Rather, we focused on creating a home culture and atmosphere of learning.*

Julia- *We have also chosen against having a designated homeschool classroom. Partly because we don't have the space, and partly because I would rather spend my money elsewhere, such as on books, experiences and life.*

We use our living room, kitchen, dining room, bedrooms. And when we travel, we use our car, airplane seats, parks, libraries, museums, historical sites and hotel rooms as well. Not having an official classroom set up in our home, has not negatively impacted our homeschool success at all.

We wanted our children to know that they could learn anywhere. They do not need to be sitting at a desk. Nor do they need walls of distracting, bright colored posters surrounding them. Many children are distracted by bright and busy surroundings and are not more engaged in learning. They actually learn better when they get to choose where to study.

Some children may choose to read comfortably situated in a chair, on the sofa, on their bed, on the floor, or even in a hammock. Does it matter where they read? Does it matter if a child writes at the kitchen table, at the hearth, on a blanket under a shady tree in the yard, or at a desk?

We live in a sensory overload world. Many children struggle to read, trying to block out distractions around them, and sometimes distractions on the page. A clean, ordered home is a great canvas to learn on. Additionally, homeschoolers get to enjoy the world beyond, as their classroom.

YOU NEED TO USE A HIGHLY STRUCTURED GRADED CURRICULUM FOR EACH CHILD

All public schools in the United States, currently use the *Common Core State Standards*. Some private schools and many home schools do not. Yet, home schooled children, on average, outperform their public school peers on standardized tests.

As reported by Barbara Nelson Pavan, in the Benefits of *Non-Graded Schools*, in 57 studies comparing age-grade classrooms (conventional public school) with non-age- grade classrooms (developmentally appropriate classrooms), they found that the age-grade classroom, only out-performed the non-age-grade classrooms 9% of the time. However, 58% of the time, children in the non-age-grade classrooms out-performed those in the conventional classroom.

Choosing to homeschool using a non-age grade approach is not just an alternate option. It has proven to be a very effective alternative option for homeschooling.

A non-age-grade classroom is structured differently than a conventional classroom. Rather than learning a set curriculum by age, children move through material at their own pace. So, it is not about a one-size fits all classroom, all moving forward at the same time. The students are not divided and moved forward by age, but by skill.

Many of the non-age-grade classrooms are either magnet schools for the gifted, grade schools that specifically chose this model, or one room school houses. In those schools, general knowledge can be learned either in a multi-age classroom or with peers of the same age.

Why? General knowledge is basically informational, and does not rely on the previous knowledge acquisition of the child, their executive function development, or their age. Then the skills are learned at the pace of the student.

CHILDREN HAVE TO BE HOMESCHOOLED FOR 8+ HOURS A DAY

Some states do have specific laws about how much time a day your children are required to be "In School", many do not. Make sure to check your state homeschool association website to know the specific laws in regards to where you live. You can also go to the HSLDA.org site for this information.

When considering how long you need to be actively homeschooling your children every day, consider the following: Not even public, private and charter students spend 8 hours a day learning, even if that is the hours they are in school. Remember, at school, children spend a decent amount of time moving from class to class, or activity to activity. They have lunch time, and recess to break up their days.

Additionally, it is important to note that it is common for teachers to assign a lot of "busy work" throughout the day. This fills in the time between when they are actually teaching. This allows the teacher the time to prep for the next lesson, grade papers, and work with students that need more help.

Many have found that it only takes about two hours in a homeschool environment, to get through the same lesson material covered, on a standard day in public school. There are many factors that go into this.

One big factor being the impact of one-on-one and one on a few teaching. This can shorten the learning time and increase the progress of the child.

For instance, a child taking private music lessons can progress further and faster in a once a week 30 minute private lesson, than in three one-hour orchestra classes a week, at school.

As we discussed in our previous book, *Answers to the Top Homeschool Questions* you should only be spending two to four hours tops, in actively homeschooling younger children. The time increases as your children get older, but then more of that time is spent in independent study time.

In states where it is required that you are "In home school" for more than the two to four hours a day, we would recommend breaking your day up.

Have recess times, lunch time, hands on activities, and field trips (library, museums, local historical sites). You can do nature walks and even throw in a documentary or two, followed by discussion. Listen to music. Create art. Cook together.

Think outside the box. But don't just turn to your own "Busy Work" to fill the time, because this often leads to child burn out. And when children shut down and burn out, moms are not far behind.

PARENTS HAVE TO BE TEACHING THE WHOLE HOMESCHOOL DAY

As we just discussed previously, you really shouldn't need to be actively homeschooling younger children for more than two to four hours a day, and older children for more than four to six hours a day. A lot of that time for older children, should be spent in independent studies.

Remember, that young children have short attention spans. Let's face it, most adults have short attention spans, too! By keeping learning segments short, both you and your child can remain fresh, and engaged in what is being taught.

Additionally, all people have a saturation point, where they stop retaining any more information. When children reach that point, you need to step back and give your children's minds a break, to refresh, and be ready to learn more. Which is why we recommend shorter lesson blocks, broken up by other learning activities.

Your children will be more engaged in their learning, and retain more when you keep each learning block, to a shorter duration.

British educator, Charlotte Mason, suggested lessons be about fifteen to twenty minutes in length, shorter if they check out, and begin to dawdle. If a child is daydreaming or shutting down, Miss Mason just moves on to another subject. Then she returns to the subject later that day, or another day, when the child's mind is fresh.

It is better to stop before they are ready to stop, and leave them wanting more, than to continue past their attention span.

It is also easier to keep learning fun when you keep lessons short like this. When learning is fun, children don't have to be pushed to learn.

Also avoid the mindset that you "Have to finish the whole lesson in one sitting." It is a lot more effective to schedule time and not content. You work on a subject for a certain amount of time each day and when the time is up, you move on, unless the child insists on more.

Really, it is good to leave your children wanting more. The tendency is to overteach. When we leave them wanting more, we light the fire for a life of learning.

This is why cliffhangers in movies, television shows and books work so well! People come back because they were engaged in the story and want to learn more.

Donna- *When I was teaching my children, if I came to a point where their attention was waning or the end of the time available, I stopped. I would then mark in the book lightly the name of the child and date. That way, the next time, I knew where to pick right up where I left off.*

Why didn't I just use a bookmark? For one, I often had several children at different places along the trajectory of the book, when working on skills. So, a bookmark would not help. Besides, bookmarks can fall out. I had thought to come back for a later lesson and erase the previous mark and leave the new one after the day's progress. Only, I forgot to do so. Now my grandchildren have used these books. They can see their name going next to their mama's name and dates.

Julia - *When I was teaching my oldest how to read, I first used a very popular reading program. The lessons in this program soon started becoming quite long and complex and my daughter started burning out. I tried to break up the lessons, to make them shorter and easier but even still my daughter began to become resistant to reading lessons, which was very disconcerting to me.*

Then I was asked if I would be willing to try out a new reading program to review on my blog.

This reading program was created to help your children learn how to read in just four weeks with short engaging lessons every other day.

I was intrigued and so were both my son and daughter. This program was just what my children needed. I did it with my daughter and her younger brother at the same time. The lessons were only 10 minutes every other day. They included music, and engaging activities.

My children enjoyed the lessons from day one and were asking for these lessons soon after. And yes they were reading in just a few weeks.

YOU HAVE TO PUSH ACADEMIC MASTERY AT EARLY AGES TO PROVE YOU ARE AT SUCCESSFUL HOMESCHOOLING

This is a holdover from a society that ignores the developmental needs of young children and devalues the important role of play. Please don't fall into this trap. Play has a vital role in child development. It is the curriculum they need.

Through play children integrate their senses, learn risk management, develop executive functions, visual pathways, attention-span, brain-body connections, manual dexterity, and more. All crucial for future learning. Why would we want to derail this important development, by focusing on early academic achievement?

Consider supporting healthy development and laying a good foundation. When developmental needs are ignored or overshadowed by academics, developmental benchmarks can be delayed. Then, when they need the attention span, the self-regulation, impulse-control, or manual dexterity, it won't be developed to where it needs to be. Then academics can be stalled.

We encourage parents to focus on development and a foundation now, so children will be able to progress academically, at the right time.

You can have measurable appropriate success along the way, when you support their development and go at their pace. We encourage you to take the time to create your homeschool business plan. We outlined how, in our first book, *A Beginner's Guide for Homeschooling: How to Setup a Successful Homeschool.*

We encourage parents to not compare children. Not with siblings and not with age-mates. Each child is different. Allow them to learn at their own pace.

There is a huge difference between an accelerated learner that seems to inhale knowledge, and a child who is hothoused. An accelerated learner is internally driven to learn and will surprise you. They learn on their own, without you needing to grab a curriculum. Also, they learn without you having to sit them down for lessons, flash cards, learning apps, and worksheets. A hothoused child, like plants in a hothouse, is one who is forced to bloom out of season. These hothoused children are taught early and pressured to learn, often before they are ready.

The accelerated learner will tend to keep ahead throughout their years in learning.

Why? Because they are internalizing and using the knowledge, not just storing it and retrieving it for tests. The hothouse child often struggles from the stress and pressure to perform. They often learn for a test, then forget as they learn new information for the next test.

When we think about pushing early academics on children, we are reminded of the classic Little Men,The sequel to Little Women by Louisa May Alcott. In the beginning of this book, she describes each of the children living at plumfield (the school Jo and her husband created together). We would like to share what she wrote about one particular child.

"Billy Ward was what the Scotch tenderly call an "innocent," for though thirteen years old, he was like a child of six. He had been an unusually intelligent boy, and his father had hurried him on too fast, giving him all sorts of hard lessons, keeping at his books six hours a day, and expecting

him to absorb knowledge as a Strasburg goose does the food crammed down its throat. He thought he was doing his duty, but he nearly killed the boy, for a fever gave the poor child a sad holiday, and when he recovered, the overtasked brain gave out, and Billy's mind was like a slate over which a sponge has passed, leaving it blank.

It was a terrible lesson to his ambitious father; he could not bear the sight of his promising child, changed to a feeble idiot, and he sent him away to Plumfield, scarcely hoping that he could be helped, but sure that he would be kindly treated. Quite docile and harmless was Billy, and it was pitiful to see how hard he tried to learn, as if groping dimly after the lost knowledge which had cost him so much."

Wow, what a warning. Now we are not saying that if you push your children into academics too hard and too fast that they will get sick and wake up permanently damaged like in the story above. We are saying that pushing early academics can definitely cause negative effects on your children that could damage or hinder their development in very tangible ways.

Remember, in Finland, children go to play based kindergarten at age six. So, they are not teaching them to read until they are seven. Seven is years later than Americans start. However, At fifteen years-old, Finish children far outperform American children on the Program for International Assessment (PISA). America's trend to teach younger and younger is not moving our children, to be better prepared when they leave high school.

Studies of the federally funded Head Start preschool programs have shown that children do gain an early advantage. However, they often lose that advantage by the end of third grade. So, why risk it?

HOMESCHOOL CHILDREN ARE DISADVANTAGED BECAUSE THEY DON'T HAVE ACCESS TO FACILITIES AVAILABLE AT PUBLIC, PRIVATE AND CHARTER SCHOOLS.

Public schools, charter schools, and private schools often have expensive labs, such as science labs and computer labs. They have shops, such as home economics rooms, wood shops, auto shops, and some even have homebuilding shops. Also, most of these schools have choirs, orchestra, and drama departments and full stages to perform on. These are all great resources available to their students.

It is thought by many, that comparatively homeschool students are deprived of a top notch education, because they do not have the same access to such facilities. However, we would respond that though homeschoolers do not have these same facilities, on such a grand scale, parents can still teach these same subjects, in powerful and impactful ways.

You may not have an auto shop, but you have a garage. You may not have a home ec room, but you have a kitchen. You may not have a sewing room, but can sew in the dining room or at the kitchen table. Though you may not have a science lab, many of the experiments that children do before college, can be done in the kitchen.

Donna- *When I was in elementary school, I was a Junior Girl Scout. My mom was divorced and working full time. But she offered to teach our large troop how to cook and earn the Cooking Merit Badge. Only the place where we met, did not have large enough facilities, and neither did our home. Mom went down to the intermediate school, and asked the*

Home Economics teacher permission to use the Home Economics classroom. The teacher said yes, as long as we cleaned up and took care of things. Well, we had a very successful cooking class!

While I was in junior high school, I visited a friend who was building a boat in their backyard. Every time I visited, I helped build the sailboat. When he finished the boat, he transported the boat to the bay, and launched it.

We have a neighbor, a teacher by profession, and he was also a master electrician. He took each of his teens with him, and one-on-one taught them electrical work. By the time they graduated from high school, they had the experience and knowledge to do electrical work.

I had a couple students, sisters, in a girl's college prep class, I taught. Their father was building their home. Both of the girls worked alongside their dad and learned everything from foundations, to wiring, to plumbing, to roofing, to drywall and finish work. Yes, the home was beautiful and passed inspection. This went on their high school transcript!

- *Home Building 101*
- *Homebuilding – Electrical*
- *Home Building - Plumbing*
- *Home Building - Drywall Installation*
- *Home Building - Roofing*

We had several homeschoolers in our neighborhood and a few public school girls who played the violin. They got together and created their own group. They added an adult that played the viola and one that played the harp. They held a Sunday concert on the lawn of the home of one of the girls. They invited the neighborhood. Each introduced their favorite piece and the rest joined in and played the piece with them.

There are men in the neighborhood with woodshops. They are tickled when youth show interest and are often willing to work with them on projects.

I have known homeschoolers that also learned animal husbandry and raised a flock of chickens. We were one of those families. We have known other homeschool families that raised bees.

Many schools are now having children grow gardens. Many homeschoolers do the same. Even those who live in town homes, condos, and apartments, and take advantage of balconies and window sills to grow food in containers.

Additionally, If you reach out to your local school, they may let your children participate in certain classes and extra curricular activities in Junior High and High School.

Julia - *I shared this before, but when I was in the 11th Grade I really wanted to participate in a school play with my friends at our local High School.*

My friends in the drama department encouraged me to speak to the drama teacher who agreed to let me try out for the upcoming play even though I was a homeschool student. I tried out, made call backs and got a part in their full production of As You Like it. I also participated in a few other smaller productions that year much to my enjoyment.

Yes, homeschoolers don't have the same access to grand facilities, as students at public, private & charter schools, but that doesn't stop them from learning. We just have to think outside the box, a bit.

Addressing Common Homeschool Misconceptions

5. MISCONCEPTION: HOMESCHOOL CHILDREN CAN'T COMPETE ACADEMICALLY WITH THEIR PEERS

This misconception is based on the assumption that if a child were in school, that they and their age-mate peers, would all be at grade level. This is not the reality.

Just know that there is a difference in what is taught each year, and where children actually are educationally. Only 36% of American students are reading at grade-level or above at the end of fourth grade. However, as stated before, on average, homeschool children typically outperform their public school peers on standardized achievement tests.

Before common core, public school children were not standardized tested before the end of third grade. They had found testing before then, to be unreliable, due to rapid changes in development in the first eight years. Common Core did not change the fact that children still go through rapid changes in the early years. These added tests add stress and are not reliable. However, the real point here is that there is a wide range of development in children, and it is uneven during the grade school years.

Many homeschoolers delay academics until after kindergarten, while building the scaffolding for learning. When a child is ready, lessons are easily learned. When a child is not ready, it takes longer to learn. So, homeschoolers may start later, but they do fine.

Did you know that, in the 1870's till about the 1930's, children in one-room school houses were not taught anything but the most basic of math (in everyday context at home), until the seventh grade, which was about fifteen years of age.

They tended to start school at eight or nine. Then, in the seventh grade, they would master all the math through pre-algebra and business math, all in one school year. School started after the harvest and ended before spring planting. And school was closed during the most bitter part of winter. So, many were in school about twelve weeks a year.

Why did they do it this way? Because, at that age, brains were developed enough to fully understand and comprehend the math equations. Children also had years of context, of living math at home. This context, coupled with a more developed brain, made formal math much easier to learn, and in a shorter time. *We actually have two official math premiers from this time period, that shows this.*

The next year, students would get to choose, to learn either Surveying or Euclidean Geometry, which is Algebraic Geometry. Oh, and the tests they took were not multiple choice. They actually had to KNOW their Math, or fail.

Think about the public school classroom. On average, about one-third of the children in school are proficient at grade level or above. School curriculum is divided over twelve years, plus preschool and kindergarten. Children the same age are taught the same thing, whether they are ready or not.

Often children are moved to the next grade, without having mastered the skills taught in the last grade. This can leave them ill prepared to learn new concepts. Also they are not prepared to build new skills, because they do not have the prerequisite skills developed yet. Thus they fall ever behind and start to lose confidence. In many cases, children begin to hate learning and mentally check-out, long before they can drop-out.

In homeschool, children have the opportunity to learn at their pace. They do not move forward until they have actually mastered the skill they are learning. This is beneficial, as they are actually moving forward and progressing. This builds confidence and excitement in these children to continue learning. Also, for accelerated learners, they are not frustrated by being held back, they can go at their pace.

Studies show that on average, homeschool children outperform their peers, even though many do not use the same curriculum or educational model. Homeschoolers have been getting into college and doing quite well for decades.

HOMESCHOOLED CHILDREN ARE ALWAYS BEHIND

Honestly, this is a misconception that has always bothered the both of us. Whenever we hear someone say that a child is behind, we have to hold our tongue to not say, "Behind What?"

The myth of the behind child, has harmed the learning, development, and self confidence, in too many children. This myth is pervasive even in school, where only a third of children test proficient or higher in reading going into high school. Learning is not a race or a destination. It is a journey. One that we all take at a different pace.

People process information differently and have natural affinities to certain subjects depending on which brain processes they have developed and are accustomed using. This isn't a bad thing.

Julia- *True story. At the end of third grade, I was two years below reading level. My teacher was very vocal about her worry that I had a learning problem. This was despite being above grade level with every other subject and in a gifted class, for math.*

Thankfully, my parents didn't worry and just encouraged me to continue to learn and grow. They said that when I was ready, I would advance in reading. In the meantime, they continued to read to me and actively discuss the books they were enjoying.

That summer I was finally ready. I worked on my reading. When I went back to school I was so far above grade level in every subject, including reading, that they skipped me into the next grade. To this day, I read three to five books a week, despite my busy schedule as a full time work-at-home, homeschool mother of three.

Before labeling your child as behind, we would suggest that you step back and ask yourself, are they ready for that subject? Do they need to be taught in a different way, to help them to grasp the subject? Are they just not interested in the subject? Are they distracted, which is slowing down their learning of that subject.

Another thing we have learned over the years, is the importance of leading with our children's strengths, and not focusing on their weak spots.

When you focus on and talk about your child's weak spots, soon that is all you or your child will see. This can seriously skew yours and their perspective. It can also cause your child's confidence to plummet and lead to burn out. This can also lead to a closed mindset and a child adopting the label.

However, if you look for and focus on your child's strengths, and lead your child into learning with those strengths, you will notice they will improve across the board. This is largely due to the fact that when a child's confidence grows, they will naturally want to conquer harder subjects. For they will be confident that they can do it.

A great way to focus on your children's strengths is to do victory lists. Keep a victory list of what your child learns and accomplishes. Recognize their progress. Focus on these victories.

There is something about recognizing strengths and victories that invites people to work for more victories. Focusing on victories and strengths, helps build a can-do, growth mindset. "Just wait, if you liked that, you haven't seen anything yet!"

Almost everyone enjoys validation. We are not talking here about participation trophies, awards, or just lauding effort. We are talking about recognizing victories and areas of strength.

HOMESCHOOL STUDENTS ARE ALWAYS BAD WITH CERTAIN SUBJECTS, SUCH AS MATH AND GEOGRAPHY.

This misconception is probably grounded in the fact that many moms hated math and geography in school. Many moms can not imagine teaching these subjects.

Subjects such as Geography and History, are not skill based, but facts based. They deal with rote memorization, or working memory. Some children are naturally better with memory, than others, across all educational venues.

Also, working memory is an executive function and can improve with executive function development. They can also do more to develop their executive functions, such as working memory.

A benefit that homeschool children can have is that they are able to experience Geography. They can experience Living History museums and reenactments, not just learn from a textbook.

In homeschool, children often move at the pace of their developmental readiness. At any given time, they may appear ahead or behind in what they are being taught. The difference is, that homeschooled children are taking the time to learn, instead of moving forward by age.

By the time they are finishing their journey, for those choosing college, they usually pay the price to learn what they need to.

Learning at home offers the benefit to children that they can slow down and learn math in different ways. If one way is not working, they are free to try others. They can watch different math demonstration videos and find one that makes sense to them. Also, in life at home, homeschool children have a better opportunity to learn practical applications of math.

It is to be remembered, that homeschoolers on average outperform their peers on standardized tests. That would not be so, if they were always bad at certain subjects.

HOMESCHOOL CHILDREN ARE NOT "REALLY" LEARNING AT HOME

The important thing to addressing this misconception is first to define learning. Unless your child is locked in a dark room, they are learning. Learning is part of children's nature. Children are wired that way. From their earliest years, children naturally are taking in input and organizing that input into actual usable knowledge.

Think about babies who learn how to move, recognize people, eat, talk, navigate their world and express their needs even before they can formally speak. This natural process doesn't just end there, it continues throughout life.

Even people who never learned to read or do advanced math, who have been labeled uneducated, have been found to be very smart. Often, they learn to navigate their world, without those formal academic skills.

Many people may have this misconception, because homeschool may not look like public school. However, you have to ask yourself which is more important, looking like school, or actually learning? Many homeschoolers learn in the context of life. As they need the tools of knowledge, they learn and master them.

It is also important to acknowledge the importance and validity of street knowledge vs just book knowledge. Most public, private and charter schools put an emphasis on book learning, alone. Meanwhile, many homeschool families emphasize both book learning and practical street knowledge.

Why? Because, both book learning and hands-on street knowledge used together, will benefit the student later in the real world.

We will be going into this a lot more in books four through six in our *Homeschooling Basics* series. These books will focus on the practical applications for homeschooling preschoolers & kindergarteners, grade schoolers, and middle schoolers through high schoolers.

WHAT ARE WE MEANING, WHEN WE SAY STREET KNOWLEDGE?

When we say street knowledge, we are talking about life skills, as well as real world applications for things learned in books. What good is knowledge without insight into how to apply that knowledge? It is said that this is the difference between knowledge and wisdom.

When children learn in context, they can see how that subject applies to real life. Learning in context, helps children stay engaged in learning. Also, you avoid the commonly asked question, "Yes, but when will I ever use this?"

Additionally, there are lots of important skills and lessons not commonly taught in school. Some subjects are best taught in everyday life, such as home finances, how to fix things around the home, frugal shopping, gardening, food processing, and meal planning.

Children need to know how to become a grown up. They need to know how to navigate their community. They need to attend school boards and city council meetings with their parents. They need to learn how to participate effectively. At some point, children need to see their legislature at work.

It has been found that homeschool graduates are more active in their community, in adult life.

We find it sad how often children are not taught these things at school or at home. The result is poor life decisions, debt, and not being prepared for adult life. Now we are seeing colleges having to teach "adulting" classes.

Also, we are seeing a lot of newly wed couples who lack basic home skills, reaching out on social media, asking for help. Homeschooling offers a great opportunity for children to naturally learn these lessons alongside their formal academics, for a WHOLE education.

HOMESCHOOL CHILDREN ALWAYS DO POORLY ON OFFICIAL TESTS

As we have stated in this and the other books in our *Homeschooling Basics* series, this misconception is patently not true. Homeschool students on average, actually do better on standardized tests, than their public, private, and charter school peers.

Many homeschooled children seeking to be admitted to their selective colleges and universities of choice, do so based on their high ACT/SAT scores.

"A new study published in **The Journal of College Admission** suggests that **homeschool students** enjoy higher ACT scores, grade point averages and graduation rates compared with other college students. " Can Homeschoolers do well in College by Lynn O'Shaughnessy, CBS News.

HOMESCHOOL CHILDREN JUST PLAY ALL DAY

First of all, we would like to reiterate that play is a good thing. Children learn through play and develop important executive functions through physical and imaginative play.

Executive functions? That's their internal CEO. Think sensory integration, brain-body balance, attention span, emotional self-regulation, delayed-gratification, impulse control, working memory to name just a few. These, and more are developed through play, not through lessons or telling.

Additionally, through play, children learn how to take and manage risks, to set goals, make plans to achieve those goals and learn how to pay attention to detail and follow through on their goals. It is through play that children become inspired and dream.

When you cut out play as a main source of learning for young children, you can stunt their development and growth.

Having more opportunity for play, both structured and unstructured, may play a major role in why most homeschool children often outperform public school peers, year after year, on both social and academic measures.

As we have discussed earlier in this book, it does not take as much time in the homeschool environment to teach the same material, as in the classroom.

We have also stated and will restate that official homeschool work should be kept between 2 - 4 hours tops for younger children. And 4 - 6 hours for older, with a large portion of this longer time devoted to self-directed, interest-led, independent studies. This leaves more time for children to learn from play and naturally develop.

So, while it is a real misconception that homeschool children play all day, they do, in fact, often get in more play than many of their peers.

6. MISCONCEPTION: HOMESCHOOLED CHILDREN CAN'T GET INTO COLLEGE OR GET REAL JOBS

Nothing could be further from the truth. As we have stated before, colleges and universities do accept and often recruit, homeschool students. Most colleges actually have a homeschool specialist in their admissions department. These specialists are trained to work with homeschooled students who are seeking admittance. They help homeschooled students navigate the admissions process.

Homeschoolers can and do pay the price to prepare themselves for college, all the time. Those who desire to follow a professional path into law, medicine, dentistry, or even engineering, can and do get into good colleges.

We know several homeschooled youths who did, in fact, get into a good college, did well, and then earned advanced professional degrees.

Likewise, there are many homeschooler's, though well educated, that do not have a desire to attend college. These homeschoolers often have a specific career or trade they are more interested in.

Those homeschooled children that do not go to college, have had no problem seeking or finding their desired employment. Probably because, unless asked, most people have no idea if someone was homeschooled, or not.

And lastly, some homeschoolers decide to go the entrepreneurial path and start their own business. Often, homeschoolers start their business before even finishing school. Again, we know of several who have successfully done so, even in the high demand tech fields!

COLLEGES DON'T ACCEPT HOMESCHOOL DIPLOMAS OR TRANSCRIPTS

Colleges and universities do accept properly created transcripts and portfolios from homeschool students. We discuss how to create an official transcript in our last book, *Answers to the top Homeschool Questions.*

For the record, many colleges and universities weigh the ACT/SAT heavier than the high school transcript. This has come about, because of grade inflation. Colleges cannot look into the individual classrooms to determine how classes were taught. However, ACT/SAT questions are the same for everyone.

Then there are also about 800 colleges and universities that do not require an ACT or SAT for admissions requirements.

As for homeschool diplomas, most colleges and universities have a special admittance process for homeschool students. If there is a specific school your child is interested in attending, we recommend contacting them. Ask to speak to their homeschool admission specialist, to get the specifics on what they require.

We encourage homeschoolers to contact colleges before starting high school studies. Find out what the homeschool admissions specialist advises as subjects to study in highschool. Aslo, find out what the prospective school is looking for in students. This will help the homeschooler to efficiently navigate college prep.

Often, colleges and universities look primarily at ACT/SAT test scores. Then they look at the transcript to see what the student has studied. Then they look at student portfolios, which showcase specific talent, interests and extracurricular activities and service your child has done.

If you are concerned that your child doesn't have a high school diploma, your child can always take the GED test. A GED is a General Educational Development test.

In many states, the GED actually grants the student an official state issued diploma. In other states, the GED grants the student an equivalency diploma, which your child can include in their college application. However, many schools do not require a diploma or GED, if you have scored well on the ACT or SAT.

HOMESCHOOLED CHILDREN WON'T BE PREPARED FOR COLLEGE OR COLLEGE LIFE

Homeschool students are accepted into college and universities every year. This is because they are well prepared, and do well on the ACT/SAT tests. These students have shown to consistently perform well on their coursework, once they were admitted into college.

In the 1970s, there were about 13,000 homeschoolers nationwide. Almost four decades later, before COVID, there were over two million families homeschooling in the United States.

Homeschoolers who were the torch bearers over the past decades, have led the way for others to follow. This vanguard of homeschooled college students shows that any student who prepares, can get into desired colleges and universities. They have also shown the way to get well paying jobs or to create businesses, themselves.

As for colleges, did you know that most changed their admission policies years ago, at the end of the last century? By 1993, homeschool was legal in all fifty states. Colleges began to admit the growing number of homeschool applicants. Homeschoolers going to college is not a rare thing. It is actually quite common.

Many homeschoolers engage in concurrent enrollment and receive dual college and high school credit for the same courses. Some homeschoolers do highschool studies in junior high, and then begin college early, full time. Others enter college early on their ACT score alone, without stopping to pick up a high school diploma.

WHAT ABOUT BEING PREPARED FOR COLLEGE LIFE?

Homeschoolers are often ahead of the game, when it comes to academic preparedness. Which is why so many colleges and universities accept homeschool applicants. Some top tier colleges even recruit homeschoolers.

As for the social side of college life, preparedness is a matter of parenting and home culture, regardless of where the child was educated, be it home, public, charter, or private school. We discuss in depth how to create an effective home culture in both of our previous books in the *Homeschool Basics* series.

CHILDREN WON'T BE ABLE TO GET A JOB WITHOUT A HIGH SCHOOL DIPLOMA

Homeschooling is a legal option for schooling in every state in America, and has been since 1993. Which means your homeschool diploma is legal.

Most entry level jobs only ask on your application, if you graduated high school. To which, homeschool graduates can honestly respond, "Yes." Some jobs may ask what the name of your school was or for more information.

This is where your homeschool branding comes into play. We recommend that when you set up your homeschool, that you take the time to do your homeschool branding, just as you would for your own business.

We walk you through how to brand your school in book 1, *A Beginner's Guide for Homeschooling.* This branding includes choosing an official homeschool name, mottos and designing a logo, even if something very simple. You will use this branding for all your official homeschool documents and correspondence.

Since, not every person or company understands the legalities of homeschooling, having an official school name, logo, transcript and diploma, are wise.

Do you need help knowing how to create an official homeschool transcript and student portfolio? Don't worry we walk you through how to create these in book 2, *Answers to the Top Homeschool Questions.*

HOMESCHOOLED CHILDREN WON'T BE PREPARED FOR THE REAL WORLD

There are some homeschool families that have more polish than others. This can also be said for families who send their children to public, charter, and private schools.

The amount of preparedness for the real world depends on the family, and the ways parents choose to prepare their child, outside of homeschooling.

- Do you teach your children how to participate in respectful and thoughtful conversation or are they learning to talk over each other or speak down to each other?

- Are your children broadly educated, so they have something to say, and can articulate their thoughts clearly and logically?

- Do you teach your children diplomacy, or are your children learning to manipulate and control others?

- Are your children developing a good solid work ethic, or are they mostly focused on entertainment?

- Are you teaching your children how to manage money, or is money managing them?

- Are you teaching your children compassion, or indifference?

- Are you teaching your children basic life skills, or will they need adulting classes in college?

- Are you teaching your children the multitude of ways of participating in our form of government and being effective? Or are they learning they only have two options, voting and protests?

All of the above questions are best addressed in the home and unlikely to be lessons from school, to prepare for the real world.

Homeschool has really taken off in the past three decades and continues to increase.

Literally, millions of homeschooled adults are married, raising families and working. Unless you already know that someone was homeschooled, it is doubtful you would be able to pick them out. Nor would you be able to pick them out by profession.

Addressing Common Homeschool Misconceptions

7. MISCONCEPTION: HOMESCHOOLING IS TOO EXPENSIVE

This is also something we cover in both of our previous books in the *Homeschooling Basics* series. However, it is important we address it here, as well. As this is a common misconception that holds many parents back from homeschooling their children.

The truth is, yes homeschooling can be expensive. If you are setting up an actual classroom in your home, buying lots of supplies, tools, computers, boxed curriculums for each of your children, participating in multiple co-op extra curricular activities, and buying memberships to local museums, aquariums & zoos, then yes, it can become way too expensive, without some sort of financial assistance.

However, it really doesn't have to be. You don't need to turn an entire room in your home into a classroom with desks and everything. Children learn just as well around the kitchen table.

You don't need to buy loads of school supplies. A couple binders, & notebooks for each child along with pens, crayons, colored pencil, glue, rulers, calculators, and a couple reams of paper, etc., are sufficient to get started. You can often find these basic supplies on sale during the back to school season.

Curriculum, memberships, and school tools, such as computers, tablets, globes, maps, microscopes, telescopes, etc,. are often on sale, or can be saved up to purchase. We provide some creative ideas for how to earn, budget, or save for such items, in our first book, *A Beginners Guide for Homeschooling*.

YOU HAVE TO BUY THE TOP (OFTEN MOST EXPENSIVE) CURRICULUMS TO BE SUCCESSFUL

There are a lot of curriculums out there. They come in all shapes and sizes. From all inclusive curriculums to curriculums that focus on a specific subject, such as math, reading, writing curriculums. Some curriculums are printed and others are digital.

Sometimes, parents buy a curriculum that everyone is talking about. However, we would warn you that just because everyone is talking about it, does not mean it will be a fit for your family.

Often, parents fall in love with the popularity, the look or the rigor without considering what their children are ready for, or what their personalities will thrive with.

In book one, *A Beginner's Guide for Homeschooling*, we talk you through how to find the right kind of curriculum, to meet your family's needs. Once you know what kind of curriculum you need for your family, you can then narrow down which one you want to get.

Julia - *We actually use parts of various curriculums and educational resources for our custom-fit homeschool each year. Some of the curriculum like Power of an Hour and 4Weeks2Read cost money.*

Other resources that we use like Sheppard Software, and Typing.com are free. And since we already pay for popular streaming services like Amazon Prime, Netflix and Disney+ we have access to some great documentaries. Add to this fun hands on learning and science activities that we make ourselves or find on Pinterest and we are set without spending a fortune.

Personally, we would use many of these educational resources, even if our children were not homeschooled. We would do so, to supplement their education in a more fun and engaging way.

YOU NEED TO BUY A LOT OF EXPENSIVE SUPPLIES AND TOOLS TO PROPERLY TEACH AT HOME

There is no doubt about it, there are a lot of amazing school supplies and tools available to purchase for your homeschool. These tools and supplies can definitely enhance your school. However, many of them can be quite expensive.

There are computers, tablets, printers, laminators, microscopes, telescopes, calculators, sweet office furniture, whiteboards, furniture for a homeschool room or office, home economics equipment, shop equipment, art supplies, science kits, P. E. equipment, and musical instruments that you can purchase for your homeschool.

One thing to note however, is that you often will not need or use all the above at the same time or even ever. Which means, these supplies and tools do not all need to be bought upfront when you start homeschooling.

If your children are younger, we would recommend that you start simple, when it comes to school supplies and tools. Then you can save and budget for the more expensive tools, **as needed**. This will help you avoid buyer's remorse and make your homeschool more budget friendly.

Some tools you may want to buy new, I am personally particular about my computers and tablets. While other tools, which you won't use as often, may be more cost effective, and money wise, to buy second hand. You may even be able to borrow, share, or rent these less often used tools, saving you money. The money saved along the way, you can use elsewhere.

YOU HAVE TO SPEND A LOT ON EXTRA CLASSES AND ACTIVITIES TO SUPPLEMENT WHERE YOU LACK AT HOME

The homeschooling movement has had exponential growth, in this century. In the 20th century, parents would talk to local artists and other people with special skills, to set up classes for interested youth.

Donna - *When we lived in Colorado, a local university professor offered to teach a homeschool science class. Parents loved this idea and worked together to make it happen.*

In the 21st century, many parents share their talents with the homeschool community, through offering classes and special interest activities, or through co-ops.

Many 21st century homeschool parents start classes in their homes, co-ops, commonwealth schools, and now, homeschool pods. They teach art, coding, ACT prep, math, writing, science classes, and other areas of interest.

Some parents start book groups, choirs, musical groups, and classes in how to use parliamentary procedure. Still others, teach life skill classes, such as sewing, cooking, car repair, and gardening.

With homeschooling, you can participate in this smörgåsbord of classes and learning experiences. These classes can help cover subjects you may feel lacking in. You may also choose to do this to give your children additional social interaction.

While classes are great, every interest does not need to be a class. There is a lot to be gained from learning skills in everyday life. You would be surprised at how many of these important skills you actually know and don't need to outsource.

Taking classes can be fun, signing up for a lot of classes can, on the other hand, derail your homeschooling. This is why we advise you to be choosy in what out of home classes and activities you participate in.

THE ONLY WAY TO AFFORD HOMESCHOOL IS IF YOU DO A CHARTER THAT REIMBURSES YOU FOR YOUR EXPENSES.

A charter school is usually a public school, with more parental input and less funding. Though they often have more flexibility than public schools for curriculum, they are still subject to the state school board and their directives.

Some states let charter schools have on campus, full time students, and also oversee distance learning for other students. This distance learning comes in different forms, including home selected and mostly, home administered learning.

These programs often offer special classes, testing, and social opportunities. While these charter schools usually advertise to the homeschool community, when they offer online options and curriculum/supply reimbursement, they are in fact, still a public school offering. Again, because these are public schools, using public funds, they are subject to changes made by the school board.

Yes, some of these charter schools that advertise to the homeschool community, do so saying, that if you don't like our curriculum, we will let you purchase your own and we will reimburse you.

However, this comes with strings attached. You are still subject to all the mandates and required subject content from the state. Only certain other curriculums and school materials are accepted for reimbursement. You are also subject to class hours, tests and reports to teachers or advisors, for each student. Reporting is usually on-going, and not once a semester. Even when you find and get reimbursed for your chosen curriculum, there are often busy work requirements. These are often, outside your curriculum, and must be turned in weekly or bi-weekly. Remember, this is also a contractual agreement.

Many people like participating in these charter school at home programs, especially for the $$ reimbursements. Others have found that the requirements are not worth the money.

Usually, under state laws, the thing that distinguishes home schooling from public schooling, is who pays for it.

Homeschooling is not determined by where students receive their learning instruction, or who does the teaching. Because homeschoolers are not funded by the state, they have more freedom to structure home learning in the best way to meet their family's needs. They can teach what their children are ready for and what their children need. They can choose how they want to teach their children, within the state's laws.

HOW DO YOU AFFORD HOMESCHOOL WHEN NOT REIMBURSED THROUGH A CHARTER SCHOOL?

Many parents, of modest means, have provided wonderful homeschooling to their children and done so on a shoestring, without state funding. Indeed, with a library card, or internet (over 82% of US homes have an internet subscription), and the world around us, one can homeschool very well, for very little.

For the 18% of Americans without internet subscription, most public libraries have computers and internet access for the public to use.

There are many great online homeschool resources that are free or very inexpensive. Here are a few of the free educational resources we have used and recommend.

SHEPPARD SOFTWARE

(https://www.sheppardsoftware.com/) is a free website that offers educational games and resources for a variety of subjects. We particularly love their Geography

KHAN ACADEMY

(https://www.khanacademy.org/) is a free online school (PreK - 12th grade) which offers a series of courses for both core subjects as well as selective electives such as programming and creative writing.

GUTENBERG

(https://www.gutenberg.org/) What if you do not have a library near, or one that has a lot of books? Gutenberg has a plethora of much loved great works that are now in the public domain. These books are available in various formats to be easily read on different electronic devices.

LIBRIVOX

(https://librivox.org/) Librivox is a site that provides FREE audio books. So, you can listen while you rest your voice! Listen while you drive. Listen while you eat.

PINTEREST

(https://www.pinterest.com/) Pinterest is a visually curated site, leading to websites with a wealth of knowledge and how-to instructions. Many free or very inexpensive. You can find great educational printables, activities and experiments on Pinterest to use in your homeschool.

YOUTUBE

(https://www.youtube.com/) Youtube has a wide variety of learning content. You can find Classical Music and different genres of music. You can also find Math, Science, Art, and Music Lessons. Of course, Youtube is famous for their How-to videos.

Seriously, if you don't know how to do something, you can usually find a youtube video to help you. Such as cooking, calligraphy, sewing, car repair, how to build a business, how to write a five paragraph essay, and more.

DOCUMENTARIES

Amazon Prime, Disney +, Netflix, Hulu & Youtube
You can find some great documentaries available on each of these streaming services. There are several on history, animals, space, science, geography and more. You can find a list of over 55 great documentaries found on these popular streaming services on Julia's blog (https://thequietgrove.com/55-educational-documentaries-available-to-stream-on-netflix-amazon-prime-disney-youtube/)

FREE LOCAL RESOURCES

Be sure to also consider the wide variety of wonderful free opportunities for learning in your community. Cities often have several free days each year, for admission to major educational attractions, such as the zoo, the botanical gardens, and museums.

Many cities have free concerts in the park and free cultural fairs. If you live near a university, they often offer free concerts and dress rehearsals. There are probably a lot more free opportunities than you realize.

Then there is nature. Step out your front door. There is so much science that can be learned for free. Nature studies is the springboard into natural science and it can be had for free.

Here are some of our favorite curriculums and educational resources that cost money, but are affordable and very worth their price.

POWER OF AN HOUR

(https://mentoringourown.com/power-of-an-hour-overview/) This is an all-in-one, grab and go, open and grow family style curriculum. The Power of an Hour covers both core subjects of Literature, Math, Science, World / US Geography, World / US History, and Language Arts (Spelling, Grammar, Roots, and Affixes), as well as the Fine Arts of Art, Music, and Poetry.

This curriculum takes about one hour a day to teach! You can teach all your children together. Affordable too! Homeschool your family for as little as the cost of a hot and ready pizza, a week.

LEARNING DYNAMICS

(https://4weekstoread.com/?rfsn=2422155.02b3eb) This amazing reading program will have your children reading in just 4 weeks with only a 10 minute lesson every other day. It utilizes music, flash cards, activities and a whole library of books that are introduced to your children as a few at a time as they learn new letters to build confidence from actually reading as they learn.

It is developmentally designed to teach your children to read. Best of all kids love it!

MATH ANTICS

(https://mathantics.com/) These are fun and clear videos and to help children learn basic math and Beginning Algebra. Many videos are on Youtube and are FREE. However, the website has an affordable, full program of math exercises, worksheets, etc.

LINKED IN LEARNING

(https://www.lynda.com/) is a site that has several online courses for many high demand tech skills from how to use specific tech programs, to programming, graphic design, photography editing and more.

Some libraries (like the Provo Library in Utah) offer free access to Lynda for those who have a library card. So, check with your library before you purchase any of the online classes.

HOMESCHOOL DISCOUNTS

More and more companies are now extending their student and teacher discounts to homeschoolers which is awesome. Many venues, likewise, offer a homeschool group discount if you set up a large enough group to attend.

We would also advise keeping your eyes out for discount days at local venues. Most have a few a year.

8. MISCONCEPTION: HOMESCHOOL MOMS HAVE NO LIFE

This is actually something that many mother's struggle with, no matter where their children go to school. The fact is, having children is a big commitment, especially when it comes to their education. If you want your children to thrive in their learning, then you have to be involved, no matter where your children are educated.

For those with children in public, private or charter schools, this means dropping off and picking your children up from school, volunteering in your children's classrooms, overseeing nightly homework, and school projects, as well as time spent taking care of your children. For homeschool moms, this means teaching, overseeing study time, meals, and field trips.

Many parents overschedule their family's time. This is culture wide, and does not depend on where their children are educated.

Overscheduling can impact moms, who transport and support their children, and can bring added stress to both moms and their children. With this mindset of living every moment for their children's wants and needs these moms worry that if their children are home with them all day, they won't have any time for themselves.

Really this is not the case. Many homeschool moms actually find that they have more, not less time for themselves. The first step to making sure mom has a life, is to simply not overschedule.

It's a simple truth, that homeschool moms have a life, if they plan a life. No matter where you children are educated, you do not find time, you prioritize time. You have to prioritize renewal. Some of this may be in rising before your family, when you have no interruptions.

Also, consider having a quiet time in the afternoon, so your children are not overstimulated. During this quiet time moms can focus on personal needs.

Donna - *My mom had an artist's heart. She was always trying to improve her art. She took me to class with her when I was a preschooler. The class gave me a canvas, a palette, oil paints and brushes. I fell in love with art and mom developed her art. This showed me I could pursue interests and take my children alone, enriching them too.*

*I wanted to read classics for a class. I did not want to take time away from my children. So I read the classics aloud to them. I wondered what my toddler was getting out of this. She was building on the floor, as I read. One day, she came to me in the kitchen and asked, "Mommy, when are you going to read **Jane Eyre**?"*

I wanted and needed to get out and get exercise. My children were too young to leave alone. So, I took them with me. I let them run ahead and back to me. We learned to love family walks together.

While I do take my children to museums and other venues, as my mom did me, I sometimes go alone. Sometimes, on a Saturday or an evening, when dad is home, I did do something to replenish. I love to go to a gallery or museum. Because I grew up around oil paintings, the smell of oil paints is a comfort smell, and boosts my mood.

So, yes you can have a life, sometimes with your children, and sometimes alone.

HOMESCHOOLERS STAY HOME ALL DAY

Some homeschooler's are homebodies, just like many public, charter, and private school moms are homebodies, as well. Other homeschool families spend a lot of time out and about.

This is really all about personality and preference. Honestly, one of the best things about homeschooling is that the world becomes your homeschool.

If you find yourself going stir crazy at home, then take your children to a library, a museum, on a nature walk, or a place of interest. Call up another homeschool friend to meet up with you so you can have mom time while your children can enjoy social time with friends.

Unless you are under a government enforced stay at home order, you do not have to stay home.

WHAT CAN YOU DO IF YOU ARE REQUIRED TO STAY HOME?

Consider a staycation, A staycation is a themed vacation at home. They can be fun and educational too depending on your theme.

You could pick a country, look up foods to cook from that county, listen to the music, dance to their music. Learn about their art. Watch documentaries about famous people from that country. Enjoy travel videos from that country. Try your hand at a craft from that country. Do virtual tours and have fun with this.

Switch up your homeschool lessons, to do more hands-on activities. Do family workouts, yoga, or meditations. Have family game nights and movie nights to balance homeschool days. Build forts, start new fun books as a family. Create or celebrate fun or funkie holidays, such as, talk like a Pirate Day, Mad Tea Party Day, Pancake Day, and Pi Day. There are fun things associated with every day of the year.

Whatever you do, staying home and moaning about what you cannot do, helps no one. Teach your children how to thrive! Use your imagination, and make your home a haven, not a prison.

WHAT MOMS DO DURING THE DAY WITH THEIR OWN EDUCATION ISN'T AS IMPORTANT AS THE CHILDREN'S EDUCATION

Some vocal people are under the misconception that if you homeschool, you need to focus every moment of your day on your children. That it is selfish, or impractical to spend time on yourself working on improving your own education.

However, one of the best things you can do to help your children gain a love and appreciation of learning is to show them how much you love learning. When your children see that you are working on your own education they will be inspired to do the same.

If you are intending on homeschooling for the long run, continuing your education will become a must. You will find yourself studying topics to teach your children and topics along with your children. This is natural.

Donna - *My mother was inspiring. She worked on getting a college education as I was growing up. We both graduated from college the same year. She was an example to me. So, when I felt the desire to return to college, and earn a master's degree, I knew I could. I structured my days to take care of family, home, and to homeschool, as well as do my graduate studies.*

When I was a younger mother, and homeschooling, I relearned many things, as I taught my own children. I also broadened my education while teaching my children. Homeschooling helped kindle my fire to love learning, again.

Julia- *I am a big book worm. Reading is how I relax and rejuvenate. Often my children will hear me mutter to myself, laugh, snort, sigh or growl while I am reading and ask me to share. I like to learn how to do new things from crafting to cooking to fun skills. As my children have gotten older they like to join in and learn with me.*

My husband is always studying current events, finances, politics, history and other topics of interest. As he does we like to discuss what he is learning. Our children overhear these discussions and will often join in asking questions which start some amazing conversations.

Since we both work from home, our children love to come in our room (during their free time after homeschool is over for the day) to watch us work and see what we are working on. This has inspired my children to want to learn how to do what we do.

Continuing your education, does not have to be formal and does not have to mean seeking a degree. Learning can be part of your lifestyle. You can lead the way and inspire your children, by taking charge and investing time in learning and developing talents and new skills.

Nothing is more inspiring than an adult leading the way and developing themselves. Growth is the evidence of life. Learning leads to growth and helps youtube alive!

.

HOMESCHOOL MOMS HAVE NO TIME FOR SELF-CARE OR PERSONAL DEVELOPMENT

One of the things that we discuss in *A Beginners Guide for Homeschooling* is the importance of mom care. Mom care, or self-care, is not a luxury, it is a necessity. If we aren't taking care of our needs first, we won't be able to meet the needs of our loved ones who depend on us.

We encourage moms to make sure to schedule time every day for mom care. This should be non-negotiable, when it comes to your schedule. Your self-care time does not have to be long to be effective.

An important aspect of your mom-care routine should be devoted to your personal development.

Donna - *I like to set the foundation for my day. I like to study the scriptures, write in my journal and boost my energy through exercise. I also like to make a note of things I want to do that day, as well as important commitments, and create a vision of my day. I like to read. However, many days I only get fifteen minutes, but I move forward. On warm spring to fall evenings, I enjoy a walk around the block at the end of the day, to unwind.*

In mid-day, we have a quiet time, and to have my children do so too. We all need margins in our lives. Just like a page that has type from edge to edge is difficult to read, days filled every moment make life hard to breathe.

Do you need time to deep breathe? While your children play or read, take a few minutes to do some deep breathing. You can also teach your children to take a "breather break." Stop and breathe with them.

What about exercise? What if your husband is deployed or works shifts, and is not there to be with the children when you exercise? There are new exercise plans that do not require weights or equipment and take four to seven minutes.

While your children play, or during quiet time you can take four minutes and do the four different High-Intensity Interval Training (H.I.T.) exercises, or do a seven-minute Sprint Interval Training (S.I.T.) exercises.

You could trade with a friend. You watch her children, while she exercises. Then she can watch your children while you exercise.

Another option is to consider leading your children in daily exercise, such as, yoga, H.I.T. or S.I.T. exercises. You can take them for long walks. Turn on the music and dance!

Julia- *My husband and I both work from home as well as homeschool. Since he is a morning person, he likes to get up before the rest of the family for some time to himself. I, on the other hand, am an evening person so I like to stay up just a bit later than my family for me-time.*

No matter how you spend your time or when you schedule it, the important thing is to make your mom care a priority. Even five minutes a day can make a huge difference in filling your inner well.

When our well is full, we have more energy. Furthermore, whatever is down in the well, can come up in the bucket for our families and those around us. But if we do not do self care, we get depleted and have little to give.

HOMESCHOOL MOMS DO NOT GET THE OPPORTUNITY TO SOCIALIZE WITH OTHER PEOPLE

This misconception ties in with the misconception that homeschool moms are isolated and at home all day. Seriously, this is only true if you chose for it to be. Again, this is the same, no matter where your children receive their education. Socializing is a choice and happens for those who are intentional about it.

Many moms buddy up with one or two other moms. They get together for lunches and let their children play. They may even homeschool together.

Some mothers gather with other mothers for support, in the evenings after dinner. Other moms do park days, meet up with mom friends, and let their children play.

Donna - *At one point in my homeschooling, Lenore moved into the neighborhood and she homeschooled. We had two children the same age. We got together and socialized, we walked with our children, and did field trips together. When I was down with a HG pregnancy, she stepped in and helped one child learn to read.*

When it comes down to it, mom's need to ditch the mom guilt and make time for friends. It may only be once a month. It may be more often. The key is to make it happen.

Julia- *I used to bemoan the fact that I had no close mom friends. As all my friends had moved farther away. More than anything, I wanted a bestie or two that I could talk to, and do things with.*

Yet, as I look back there were multiple times that an acquaintance would invite me to participate in a girls night or book club and I would politely decline. I knew my husband worked long hours and I didnt want to ask him to watch our children after a long day at work just so I could go have fun.

However, I eventually found myself so isolated I wanted to cry. Putting my needs consistently aside for my family was leading me to a fast breakdown. I needed a mom friend.

I spoke to my husband about it and he told me he had no problem watching over our children for me to go out. After all, I did so when he wanted to meet up with his friends. I decided that the next time someone reached out to invite me to participate in something, that I would say yes.

The very next night, I got a text from an acquaintance inviting me to join a BUNCO group she was forming. Twelve of us would get together once a month to play bunco, talk, laugh and enjoy yummy food.

I am glad I said yes, because I made some really good friends over the next two years. Even though we only got together once a month, it made a huge difference in my life.

We need other people, but to have a friend, requires being one. If you don't want to be alone, you need to put yourself out there. Believe me, we know it can be hard to do this.

BETWEEN PREPARING FOR LESSONS AND TEACHING THEIR CHILDREN, HOMESCHOOL MOMS HAVE NO TIME FOR ANYTHING ELSE

We have talked about this throughout our *Homeschooling Basics* series. Your prep and lesson times, all depend on the model and philosophy of education, you ascribe to for your homeschool.

Are you trying to do the age-grade model of education, with multiple children? Are you trying to balance a different grade curriculum for each child? Or are you teaching your children together in a non-age grade mastery model, like in the one room school houses?

Are you pushing early academics on your young children? Or are you letting them learn through play and working with you on your projects throughout the day?

Are you relying on worksheets and busy work that requires lots of oversight and prodding? Or are you keeping your homeschool day short? Are you focusing on teaching the core subjects in short yet powerful blocks, then moving on before your children's interest waines?

Think carefully about how you answer these questions.

HOMESCHOOL MOMS ARE DUMPY

Despite popular belief, homeschool moms do not all spend their days with their hair in a messy bun, wearing their pajamas or yoga pants. No more than any other mom.

You do not have to be dumpy. That is a personal choice. Either we value self-care and prioritize it, or we do not. We can make the personal choice to look our best and we can encourage that in our children. This is basic self respect.

Donna - *I attended a personal style class and another homeschool mom I knew was there. She said that she had stopped wearing functional clothing all day and dressed office casual. Functional clothing are clothing designed for a specific function, like jeans for outdoor work, a beach coverup for the beach, or a semi formal dress, for a semi formal dinner. She found that when she took the few extra moments to dress a little more professionally, and took time to groom, her children actually respected her more and responded better.*

Later, I took an elocution class with my children. The teacher invited us to not wear functional clothing shopping, but to wear business casual. Then to see how store clerks responded to us. It was night and day.

We all enjoy a casual dressed day and feel others should be able to. However, we unconsciously respond differently, when people are too casual on the job. People who are too casual are often perceived as temporary, and are not serious. So, if you don't want to be seen as dumpy, you can choose to dress and groom.

And yes, while there are some homeschool moms that may be termed dumpy, there are also some pretty chic homeschool moms. Especially, now that homeschool is becoming trending with the younger generation of moms.

The truth is, that homeschool moms, in general look like any other mom you will meet. You won't be able to distinguish that they homeschool merely from their looks.

If you don't want to be dumpy, then don't be. There is no rule that says homeschool moms, can't dress nice, get their hair or nails done or wear makeup. There is no rule that says that homeschool moms can't take time to work out and eat healthy.

Julia - *I was complaining that I had no time to work out and my husband told me that if I wanted to work out to be healthy we would make the time. He was right. I often work out while our children are watching a documentary at the end of our homeschool day, or after homeschool is done while our children are playing.*

While I love the comfort of my pajamas and loungewear, even I get up and get dressed most days, taking a few minutes to do my hair and make up. This is really about self care. If we care, we will make time to look nice

9. MISCONCEPTION: YOU CAN'T BALANCE HOMESCHOOLING WITH OTHER RESPONSIBILITIES

The truth is, homeschool parents have been balancing homeschool, with other responsibilities for over a hundred years. In fact, many became quite good at it.

Really, it all comes down to your home culture. Do you have healthy routines in place, to ensure the smooth running of your life? We go into this topic in depth in our first book in our *Homeschooling Basics* series.

Whether or not you have a healthy home culture established, can be the make or break of your homeschool.

Too often, moms try to do almost all the housework and meal prep, by themselves. That is neither necessary or advisable. While mom is working, children are playing and making more messes! If your children are home, then learning to maintain the home is part of their education! As you train your children, life gets easier to manage.

So, the balance comes through training more hands to work. This reduces the time children are just entertained, can build their character, can strengthen relationships, and lighten your load.

For more information on how to set up a healthy home culture, we highly recommend reading the chapter dedicated to this topic in our book *A Beginner's Guide for Homeschooling*.

YOU CAN'T HOMESCHOOL AND WORK FROM HOME

We have heard it said on many occasions, that someone can't homeschool, since they work from home full-time, and there is no way they could do both.

Most of these moms have dismissed the idea, largely for two reasons. First, they have not actually studied homeschooling and imagine it is doing school at home, all day. Second, they have helped their children do their homework and it was a real struggle, night after night. The thought of doing homework all day is overwhelming to consider, on top of work commitments.

In a society where mostly both parents work, homeschoolers typically have moms come home to teach the children. Many homeschool moms have side hustles, to make ends meet. Sometimes, mom works at home and has built a solid business, and they also homeschool. There are single moms who work from home, homeschool, and provide for their family. And some have both husband and wife working from home and homeschooling together.

To stay home, raise a family, homeschool, work from home, run a home business, care for a home, nurture a husband, and care for self, is a balancing act for sure. But it can be done. Self care, simple home routines, and streamlining are the foundation to build on.

Donna - *Yes, you can! I started working from home about twenty years ago. At the time, I had my youngest five children at home, eighteen, twelve, ten, five, and two. I was homeschooling and balancing a business. I wanted* *a clean home. So, I had to learn to develop simple home routines, and engage the children in helping me.*

I had to really clarify my business and streamline those routines, too. Then I looked at homeschool. I streamlined that, too. I wanted to be effective and I wanted my children to have a rich and broad education. The result was, **the Power of an Hour** *and also the Skill Development Rotations.*

Let's face it, we all only have sixteen waking hours. We can organize those hours, guard our self care, maintain a home, run a business, homeschool, and more.

Consider a laundry basket. You take a load from the laundry and it appears to fill the basket to overflow. Yet, if you neatly fold the clothes, the basket has space for more. Likewise, our life, if we create simple routines, will have breathing space too.

Julia - *Both my husband and I work full time from home while also homeschooling our 3 children. A key for balancing homeschool and work for us has been schedules. We have a set time when we wake up, start school, finish school, eat meals and go to bed.*

Our children opted to have a little longer homeschool days Monday through Thursday, to have Friday off. This allows my husband and I to get more work in on Friday, which helps with deadlines.

We do all our homeschooling in the morning, finishing our homeschool day by lunch time, unless a child wishes to do some independent study time after. This then allows my husband and I the rest of the day to work, while our children are children and play.

We do our harder subjects that require more parental oversight and assistance first thing, finishing with subjects that our kids can do more on their own, with us working nearby to assist as needed.

The biggest thing that makes homeschooling and working from home possible is we do not ascribe to the age-grade education model. Rather, we do the Mastery Model and run our homeschool like a one-room schoolhouse. We schedule time blocks for each subject and cover what we cover each day, which is often more than you would expect.

Since my husband is a morning person, he will get up really early before the family to have some personal time and get uninterrupted work done.

I, on the other hand, am an evening person. So, I tend to stay up a bit after everyone is asleep to have me time and get uninterrupted work time in.

During our after homeschool day we tag team it working and getting up to take care of any of our children's needs as needed.

It may not always be easy to homeschool and work from home, but it is definitely doable. Especially when you aren't spending your day trying to meet the needs of multiple grade based curriculums.

YOU CAN'T HOMESCHOOL AND HAVE A CLEAN ORDERLY HOME

This issue has nothing to do with homeschooling. Many mothers struggle with having a clean orderly home. This has nothing to do with where their children are educated.

If we want a clean home and children, it is up to us to train them. This all ties into your home culture. If you don't have one, you can start now. Yes, moms can have a clean orderly home, and homeschool.

Start with yourself. If you were never really taught how to run a home, you can learn. Then set simple routines. And when you learn and have your routines, you can work with and train your children to do the same.

Habit training children is not an obedience issue. It is not just giving them a list to do. Nor is it about treating a child like an employee. Habit training provides organization, structure and muscle memory, while they develop their executive functions.

Children are still developing their executive functions. They are developing their ability to set the goal do do something, to organize in their minds what to do first, to maintain focus on the details of getting things done, to self-regulate their emotions in regards to what they are doing, delaying gratification of playing, and controlling those impulses to play, instead of working.

Children are NOT born with the organization area of their brain developed. This happens throughout childhood.

Many parents think that chores are merely an obedience issue. Often, parents think that, "Hey, my child knows what I want them to do. They are physically able to do it." They believe that all they need is the right chore chart and incentive program.

These parents are usually unaware that their child complying is impacted by their child's development.

Until a child develops their executive function and initiative, in their teen years, habit training can be a God send! Habit training helps children learn and develop life patterns, before their organizational skills are developed. It is teaching them organization through patterns.

While they gain more skill and good habits, they are also developing the foundation of their developing executive functions. As their brains mature, they have these good patterns to draw on.

WHAT IS HABIT TRAINING?

Habit training is working with your children to develop good habits and routines. A habit is developed as you do the task with a child, until the child is doing it well, themselves and becomes automatic.

Habit training involves you doing it with them, because you are their pattern to follow. There are more nuances picked up in doing the chore with you, than you demonstrating a few times and then assigning. Yes, this is work, up front. However, in the long run, habit training and routines pay wonderful dividends!

Meanwhile, moms are not having to do everything themselves, and should not. The children are receiving hands-on training.

Built habits, can then be strung together into routines. These habits and routines can in turn, help keep a home orderly. We go into depth on how to habit train children in our first book, in the **Homeschooling Basics** series, *A Beginner's Guide for Homeschooling.*

YOU CAN'T HOMESCHOOL AND DEVELOP TALENTS

Homeschooling moms can homeschool and develop their talents. Many do. We know several musicians, writers, artists, graphic artists, and more who homeschool. Developing your talents while homeschooling your children, can help your children have a growth mindset. Moms who develop their talents while homeschooling, also ignite the talents of their children.

Donna - *My mom developed her art talent while raising a family, as a full time working single mom, and going to school. This helped me see that moms can develop their talents, even under non-ideal circumstances.*

The seed my mom planted by developing her art talent, grew and flourished in the heart of her child. I went to the university and switched my major to fine art. I was expecting my second child when I graduated from college. I incorporated my artist heart into my mothering and into creating our home.

For a while, I did not produce much art in the form of drawing, painting, or creating stained glass pieces. I did explore wheat weaving, embossing, soap making, beeswax candle making, cake decorating, and even quilting. I put my art into creating a family. Then through homeschooling I began to draw as we did nature studies and nature notebooks.

Then one day, after my seventh child was over a year old, I had the idea for a giant stained glass piece. My husband was out of town during the time that I had this overwhelming urge to create. I had no workshop, but I had my tools. I contacted a friend and had him place a 4 x 8 foot piece of plywood on my dining table. There I proceeded to draw out my piece. Then it sat for a month. We ate Thanksgiving and Christmas standing around the kitchen, or at the kitchen counter. This stained glass piece had both cut glass and sandblasting. I had never done sandblasting and it had been years since I had cut any stained glass.

I finally had the courage to begin. The colors were rich and beautiful. Many friends contributed to the purchase of glass. Many stopped by my home to see the beautiful progress. I quickly was aware I could spend all day playing with glass.

I had five children at home, ages 1, 4, 8, 10, and 16. My youngest was just coming out of over a year of colic. We were finally getting to a point where we could sleep through the night. I had a family to raise, I had children to homeschool, and I had a home to maintain. It was just me, as my husband would be out of town for another year. I prayed. I searched the scriptures.

I began retiring when the children retired. I woke up well-rested before them. I was able to feed my soul and exercise. Soon, we were tidying the home before bed, so we could wake to a clean house. I wanted to give my children a solid faith foundation, so we studied scripture after breakfast. I wanted them to have a great education, with classics, history, the core subjects and the arts. I wanted them to also develop solid skills.

How could I do that by myself, without help, and it not take over my day? This is where I developed the **Power of an Hour** *and the Skill Development Block of rotations. We had a rich homeschool and family life in the morning. We established routines together. Afternoon came and we had a quiet time. While the children rested, I turned to my stained glass piece. They would get up when school children came home and went to play with them. I had the afternoon until time to cook dinner for working on my stained glass piece. After we cleaned up dinner, I was working again.*

I had a friend, Lloya, that watched me develop through this. She said that in the beginning, I would say, "I wonder what would happen, if I did this?" As I progressed she said that I changed to confidence, "I can do this!" She too, had attended the same university art school before she married. She told me that building the stained glass piece on my dining room table was genius. The corner of that table was between the living room and the hall to the bedrooms. My children had to pass me to get to their rooms or the bathroom, or to emerge to the living room. As they did, they would stop and linger. We would talk. I was always available. The older three all learned to care for all the equipment, design patterns, and to cut glass.

A sandblasting class opened up at our local Michael's Craft store. I signed up for the class. My oldest daughter babysat and I learned a new skill, which I taught her too. I needed this class to finish my piece.

At one point, the design was emerging into something that looked scary. I had to remove the pieces in the middle and redraw the center of the design to flow and radiate. In the end, the piece had over 1000 pieces of cut glass and thirteen sandblasted pieces. I submitted it into a major museum exhibit. But when I saw the other artists of renown, I thought for sure my piece would not get in the show. Not only did it get into the show, it won first place in the show.

As you can see, the process of building my talent, dovetailed nicely with homeschooling. The process of doing both refined our home culture, helped me develop better routines, and helped me design the **Power of an Hour***. Really, the Power of an Hour is daily progress, it is a broad education, and it allows all of us the time to get a good education and develop our talents.*

Again, like with self-care, developing your talents while homeschooling is a choice. If it is important to you, then you will make the time for it. Yes, it may take scheduling it into your day, but you can do it.

You could even schedule family talent time where you and your children all work on your talents for a block of time every day. Whether that is practicing an instrument, working on your drawing skills, learning how to sew or even how to do some fun baking.

YOU CAN'T HOMESCHOOL AND TRAVEL

Actually, we have found that the opposite is true. Many homeschooling families do road school or travel school. Homeschooling makes travel easier. You don't have to deal with the hassle of checking your children out of school or missing important classes. You can homeschool wherever you are. When you travel and homeschool then the world becomes your classroom.

Julia - *One of the reasons we homeschool is because we travel so much. We have taken our children with us across the US and even to multiple countries in Europe. We have good friends who homeschool and travel full time, internationally. They have done so for several years.*

We have found that traveling has inspired our children to learn more. As we visit a new place, we look up information about it. We try to immerse ourselves in the people and culture. We also try to go to educational spots like museums, zoos, aquariums, gardens, historical places etc.

We have been to many museums, zoos and aquariums across our travels. Sometimes, I wondered if my children were really learning anything during these fun educational excursions. Then one day while walking through an aquarium near San Diego, California my daughter, who was only seven at the time, started pointing out various fish to my husband and telling him their names and unique things about them, without looking at the plaques. My husband thought she was making it up but then he read the plaques himself and found out she was right. He asked her how she knew this and she responded, "Really dad, this is not the first aquarium we have visited."

Right after we formally began homeschooling, we spent six months in Europe. I loved taking my children to see places like the Acropolis, parthenon, and the monasteries of Meteora in Greece, Stonehenge and

Westminster Abbey in England and Hook Lighthouse, and castle Kilkenny in Ireland to name a few. Though my children were young at the time, they still remember visiting these places. As they and other places we have been come up in our studies or books we are reading my children are always like, "Hey we've been there! I remember that!"

Often our homeschool and studies are different when we are traveling, but our children are always learning, which is what matters. In fact, we have found that traveling has made learning come to life in many ways for our children.

We would recommend that when traveling for any extended time in a different state or country to keep your homeschool papers with you. These papers show that your children are legally registered as homeschool students, back home.

Also, be aware of any specific homeschool laws in the areas you are visiting. There are some states in the US that say if you are visiting for more than one month, that you are subject to their homeschool laws. Additionally, you may be able to use your paperwork to obtain homeschool student discounts to venues you want to visit during your travels. Having official looking Homeschool Student/Teacher IDs can help with this, as well.

Neither of us have ever had any issues regarding homeschooling in the areas we have traveled, but it is always better to be safe than sorry.

Addressing Common Homeschool Misconceptions

CLOSING

We have found that many of the fears and concerns people have regarding homeschooling traces back to a belief in one or more of the misconceptions addressed in this book. In understanding the truth behind these homeschool myths, we hope to arm you with confidence and peace in your choice to homeschool your children.

Hopefully, this book will also help you address voiced criticism and concerns of your friends and family about your choice to homeschool.

If nothing else, we hope we have assured you, that homeschooling is not just an alternative educational option. It can be a very effective educational option.

Your children are not going to be disadvantaged by being homeschooled. In fact, they will probably find that they are given an edge over their peers when it comes to college and careers.

ABOUT THE AUTHORS

JULIA ANN GROVES

Julia Groves is the third of seven children born to Roger and Donna Goff. She was born in Colorado, but raised predominantly in Utah. Julia was homeschooled from 6th grade through highschool after which she attended George Wythe College. Though she did not formally graduate with a degree, she did maintain a 3.98 GPA during her studies at George Wythe and values what she learned while attending there.

Julia married her best friend Rory Groves in March of 2009 and together they have three young children. In addition to homeschooling their children, Julia and her husband also run their own business. (Rory is an illustrator and Julia runs a family lifestyle site where she enjoys creating resources for today's mom.)

In 2015, Julia and Rory sold their home and most of their possessions to travel full time with their children. They spent 6 months living abroad in Europe and then returned back to the

US. Though their travels have now slowed down and they are once again looking to settle down in a home that love of travel is still there.

As a born storyteller, Julia has always been fascinated with history, art, different cultures and meeting new people. Additionally, Julia enjoys photography, cooking, experiencing new things, teaching, reading, crafting, travel and graphic design.

DONNA GOFF

Donna Goff and her husband, Roger, are parents of seven children and have homeschooled since the 1980s. They are the grandparents to thirteen grandchildren, twelve living. Donna earned her BA in Fine Art & Design; Drawing & Painting; and earned her MA Ed in 2008 while homeschooling her youngest three children.

She has worked to give homeschool support since 1983 and has been active in presenting at homeschool conferences around the US since 1995.

Donna loves to spend time with her family, to enjoy nature with her family, and spending time with friends. In her spare time, she loves to create art, cook, sew, garden, DIY, sing, write, is an avid walker and enjoys learning new things.

www.ingramcontent.com/pod-product-compliance
Lightning Source LLC
Chambersburg PA
CBHW060039040426
42331CB00032B/1272